YACHTING
MONTHLY

Channel Havens

YACHTING
MONTHLY
Channel Havens

SECRET INLETS AND SECLUDED ANCHORAGES OF THE CHANNEL

Ken Endean

ADLARD COLES NAUTICAL
LONDON

Published by Adlard Coles Nautical
an imprint of A & C Black Publishers Ltd
37 Soho Square, London W1D 3QZ
www.adlardcoles.com

First edition 2005

ISBN 0-7136-7099-1
ISBN 978-0-7136-7099-8

A CIP catalogue record for this book is available from the British Library.

A & C Black uses paper produced with elemental chlorine-free pulp,
harvested from managed sustainable forests.

Typeset in Meridian and Helvetica Neue
Printed and bound in Singapore by Tien Wah Press Pte Ltd

Note: While all reasonable care has been taken in the production
of this publication, the publisher takes no responsibility
for the use of the methods or products described in the book.

Contents

Shingle beach at the eastern corner of
Ile Molène, North Brittany

Foreword

IT'S A FAVOURITE AXIOM among many cruising yachtsmen that epic crossings of the open ocean are easier than short coastal passages, which confront all the inshore challenges of tides, headlands, rocks and shoal waters. Ken Endean's intrepid style of cruising often takes him to parts that most pilot books don't mention. He has been writing UK and French-based cruising and pilotage articles for *Yachting Monthly* since 1977, including his popular descriptions of coastal anchorages in the early 1990s, and advanced pilotage series such as 'Reading the Surface' and 'Sail like a Local'.

Like many of us, Ken was caught between blue water dreams and the need to earn a living, but his solution can be found in the title of the first chapter in this book – Blue Water Cruising in Home Waters. As he says, you don't have to travel to tropical, trade wind locations to enjoy adventurous, inexpensive voyaging, let alone romantic anchorages. We may complain about our weather in northern Europe, but we rarely suffer extreme conditions... though, as I write these words in January, a Force 12 warning has just been broadcast for Scotland... To help us make the most of our summers, the book includes analysis of winds and waves in coastal waters. In fact, there is a close connection between weather and pilotage: when Ken writes about 'friendly rocks', he means the ones that you are glad to see when a sea mist rolls in, obliterating all the conventional transits.

The ethos of this book grew out of a series of discussions with Geoff Pack, late editor of *Yachting Monthly*, myself and Ken. A plan for a book based on Ken's articles was one of the last projects Geoff began before he died of cancer in 1997 at the tragically young age of 39. A passionate blue water sailor, Geoff had enormous respect for Ken's spirit of adventure, whether in exploring the furthest reaches of a river or creek, or in coastal rock-hopping aboard *London Apprentice*, his Sabre 27.

With *Channel Havens*, Ken shows how to discover a new way of cruising in our own 'backyard', with hardly a palm tree or flying fish in sight. Simply follow his 'less domesticated' cruising routes, and you will enjoy quiet coves, unspoilt inlets, exquisite islands and verdant, rural waterways. Sometimes, it seems, we strain so hard to look beyond the horizon at blue water dreams, that we neglect the incredible diversity of treasures on our own doorstep. This book is as inspirational, for home waters cruisers, as books by Eric Hiscock and Geoff Pack were for ocean wanderers.

Paul Gelder
Yachting Monthly

Introduction

THE WESTERN ENGLISH CHANNEL has two splendid cruising grounds that occupy the same geographical area. In the first, which includes the harbours and marinas, generations of yachtsmen have made passages between towns such as Dartmouth, Fowey, St Peter Port and Lézardrieux, directed by a dozen or more pilot books and cruising guides. Then there is the alternative, less domesticated cruising ground that is the subject of this book. It comprises sandy bays, quiet coves, wild reefs and tree-lined creeks, offering stimulating pilotage and, in some instances, the opportunity to visit places to which a boat provides the only realistic means of access. This is yachting for the enthusiast who prefers the glow of a riding light to the glare of a streetlight, and who finds a river bar more interesting than a marina sill.

A would-be explorer who has followed the exploits of the Hiscocks and other ocean wanderers may feel twinges of frustration if confined to home waters. There appears to be a choice between sailing away in search of adventure and staying behind to earn a sober living. However, even within the crowded English Channel, it is possible to indulge a taste for exploration by investigating the less-frequented parts of the coasts, islands and estuaries. This can either be an alternative style of cruising, or a means of injecting variety into the annual holiday.

Some of the alternative destinations offer pleasures that are transient, most anchorages being sheltered only from certain wind directions and some places accessible only at particular states of the tide. Nevertheless, in times past, cargoes were carried under sail to virtually every creek and coastal crevice. Vessels unloaded on to open beaches that are now monopolised by bathers; others moored at gravel hards to serve small, rural communities. Those ancient landing places remain available, provided we follow the example of the old coaster skippers by choosing our weather and working the tides. We have plenty of good excuses to look around the next headland or to steer through the gap in the trees. If there are any ghosts, they will certainly be familiar with sailing boats.

Ken Endean
2005

Blue Water Cruising in Home Waters

The following chapters represent an imaginary cruise around the western English Channel, sailing from the Solent to the Isles of Scilly before crossing to Normandy and zigzagging westward through the Channel Islands and the coastal fringe of Brittany to the Chenal du Four. Rather than visiting the usual harbours and marinas, we shall anchor in relatively unfrequented coves and quiet creeks, occasionally making dinghy expeditions into their upper reaches. This cannot be an exhaustive review of such places, because that would demand a small encyclopaedia, but it contains a representative selection to whet the appetite. Or to wet the whistle: on inland estuaries, preference will be given to any channel that leads to a pub.

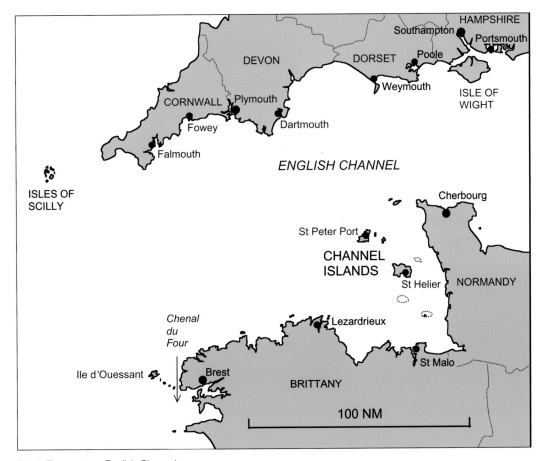

Fig 1 The western English Channel.

Worbarrow Bay, with the sea breeze fading.

When the term 'blue water cruising' was first used to denote long term, live-aboard voyaging in sunny latitudes, it had connotations of simple, inexpensive living and romantic anchorages. Some of those tropical havens have now been incorporated into the global tourist industry but many of the essentials for blue water cruising can actually be found in home waters. Northern Europe may not offer all-year warmth but neither does it breed hurricanes. During the summer months, it is possible to enjoy both the simple life and the romance of dramatic maritime scenery without even sailing beyond Ouessant.

A night spent at anchor in an open bay can be absolute magic: a driftwood barbecue on the beach, rowing back along the moon path, and phosphorescence dancing up and down the anchor chain. However, peace of mind depends upon the developing weather pattern. Coastal pilotage is also helped by a good understanding of tidal phenomena: not only the formalities of the almanac and tidal atlas but also the secondary effects that occur in shoal water and have a marked influence upon the local sea state. Chapters 2, 4 and 6 examine the behaviour of wind and water, while Chapter 9 covers certain pilotage techniques that do not feature in all sailing manuals.

A few of our stopping places demand confident boat handling and almost all require intelligent use of ground tackle. This book does not systematically discuss anchoring methods, which are adequately described in numerous other publications, but there is a short chapter on anchor types, located towards the end because it is convenient to review anchors in the context of the anchorages previously described, rather than the other way around.

It is possible for newcomers to cruising to gain an exaggerated impression of the difficulties and hazards associated with anchoring and anchorages. Most risks can be controlled by the exercise of a reasonable level of skill, supported by common sense. With my wife, Mary, I have cruised this area for a good third of a century, usually lying to anchors rather than moorings, and only twice have we been compelled to leave anchorages during the hours of darkness. The second incident could easily have been avoided, because the weather conditions were identical on both occasions and I really should have learned from the first experience. We have also struck one rock. We knew it was there but could not be sure of its exact depth, so we were proceeding very slowly and using our starboard keel as a precise sounding device. At any rate, that's my story and I'm sticking to it.

Passages and planning

Anchorages save time. When a yacht is on passage to a holiday destination, an overnight stop in a harbour usually entails a diversion from the shortest route. There is also a good chance of hassle or delay, particularly when boats are rafted together. On the other hand, if the yacht pauses in a coastal anchorage, departure can be accurately timed to catch the first of a favourable tide. While at anchor, the vessel should have remained in proper cruising order and the process of getting under way will take only a few minutes. The crew will have a realistic impression of weather and sea conditions, so decisions on sails, clothing and tactics for the next leg of the passage are likely to be well-informed. Admittedly, the anchorage may not be quite as placid as the harbour, but this is one of the principal differences between sailing and caravanning. Also, the process of going ashore to the pub may take longer, but the refreshments should taste better after the development of a modest thirst.

Any boat owner who has been accustomed to using protected moorings, as a matter of course, may find it unsettling to rely upon a small hunk of metal, hooked into an invisible patch of seabed within an open bay. Confidence comes with experience but a residual tickle of unease is an entirely healthy symptom. A yacht that is anchored behind a headland, sheltered by the arc of cliffs, is still 'at sea' and her skipper must think accordingly. Whether an anchorage is used for a short stop or regarded as a destination in its own right, each passage plan should extend to cover the period after the anchor goes down.

Charts

Anchorages save money, even if they entail the purchase of additional charts. The arithmetic is simple: for approximately the cost of a night on a mooring (expensive buoy or cheap marina), it is possible to purchase a large-scale chart, with which to explore an unfamiliar anchorage, and the chart can be used more than once. Look at it this way: a second night at anchor means 100% profit. Buy a chart and feel rich!

Apart from notes on the use of electronic position fixing, in Chapter 9, I have written in terms of manual navigation methods and conventional charts. Chart plotters and software are developing rapidly and any detailed discussion of their use would soon be out of date. In any case, someone who is accustomed to making his own pilotage decisions will feel more at home in complicated coastal waters than one who habitually takes instructions from a computer.

On the south coast of England, most of the relatively straightforward, rock-free bays can be entered with the aid of UK Hydrographic Office charts on a scale of 1:75,000 or the Imray C Series at 1:100,000. However, UKHO charts at 1:25,000 or larger scales are recommended for the intricate bits. Around the Channel Islands and France, the larger the scale, the better. For the granite rim of north Brittany, the UKHO and the Service Hydrographique et Océanographique de la Marine publish similar coasting charts at 1:50,000, but the SHOM range is more comprehensive at larger scales. The UKHO Leisure Folios, which each contain about a dozen A2-sized charts, are pretty good, although there are a few places, such as the jagged west coast of Guernsey, where the Hydrographer has evidently decided that there is insufficient interest to justify a scale adequate for exploration. He may even be right.

Sketch plans

Do not be tempted to rely upon the sketch plans in this book. Although some of them show a fair level of detail, they are simply intended to assist the reader to follow the text when the proper chart may not (yet) have been purchased. They are labelled: 'Not to be used for navigation' and with good reason: elements that are not relevant to the text have been simplified or omitted: undersea contours and most submerged rocks are not shown and there are very few depths or drying heights. Most lights have been omitted because their characteristics and locations change more frequently than other navigational features. Before even contemplating an after-dark arrival or departure, a skipper should always refer to an up-to-date chart and/or list of lights.

The sketch plans are drawn 'North up' and their content generally follows conventional chart notation, but with more colours on buoys, and beacons and on foreshores where rock is shown as dark brown, mud light brown and sand yellow. In a later chapter, the reader is warned that some areas of sand have a generous sprinkling of stones. White buoys indicate moorings, possibly available for visitors but which may obstruct the traditional anchorages.

The plans do indicate a few things that cannot be found on the official charts. Examples include certain deep pools, and rocks, where the UKHO or SHOM merely show drying sand. These features are drawn, and described in the text, because we have seen them. Some of them may not be permanent, however, and later chapters address the changing nature of parts of the seabed and foreshore.

There are also several places where the research for this book uncovered obvious errors on existing charts. These have been reported to the UKHO but the only safe assumption is that other, unsuspected errors are likely to exist, somewhere. This is not a good reason to give up cruising, or to avoid intricate waterways, but a reminder that a competent skipper does not regard any source of information as infallible.

Regulations

Off the coasts of Britain and France, waterborne activities are subject to some legal restrictions, including routeing controls, exclusion zones, nature reserves, etc. This book does not include full details of such prohibitions, the number and scope of which is likely to increase. Readers are advised to consult charts, Notices to Mariners, almanacs, harbour offices and notice boards in order to keep up to date. Customs formalities are, at present, most likely to affect yachts sailing between and around the Channel Islands.

Knowledge

I have assumed that the reader has a working knowledge of boat handling, meteorology, tides and basic navigation, including the use of transits and bearings. Rather than repeat the information that is covered by many other publications, the chapters that deal with these topics concentrate on the aspects that are particularly relevant to inshore pilotage and temporary anchorages. Similarly, there is little comment on cruising between A and B; we are mainly concerned with what happens on arrival at B.

Coastal Winds and Currents

When moving air and water encounter solid land, their behaviour becomes erratic. Winds may fade, or they may strengthen. Currents may go round in circles. It is all perfectly logical but it appears complicated. The skipper who gets the hang of these coastal quirks will be much happier than the one who relies solely upon the broad-brush weather forecast and the neat arrows in the tidal atlas.

Winds and shelter

Of all the factors affecting the safety of an anchored yacht, the most important is the next wind shift. Never mind rocks, sand banks, kelp or strong currents: they are tolerable, in varying degrees, as long as the wind is blowing off the shore. If a fresh or strong wind swings and blows directly on to the beach, then the right time to leave was before it happened. For security, please do not rely on super anchors, depth alarms or other fancy hardware but do pay close and continuous attention to the weather.

Fortunately, weather for anchoring is slightly more predictable than weather for sailing. When contemplating a passage over open water, we hope for a favourable wind direction but our safety is more likely to be affected by wind strength, which is difficult to forecast accurately. The meteorologists' estimates are approximations and a minor kink in the isobars can turn a force 5 into a force 7. On the other hand, in a reasonably well-sheltered anchorage, an unexpectedly strong blow can usually be accommodated and it is the wind direction that is most important. Given information on the position and movement of the nearest depression, it should be possible to make an adequate assessment of probable wind shifts; an estimate of direction need not be precise, provided that the wind continues to blow off the beach.

On the south coast of England, the most familiar weather pattern in summer is that associated with depressions approaching from the Atlantic and tracking across or to the north of Britain. For each depression, the wind typically backs towards south before strengthening and veering to south-west, west and perhaps north-west. If a yacht is anchored in an east-facing bay when the wind is south-west, it should remain sheltered as the depression passes. Then, as the cold front clears through, there may be an opportunity to set sail in an offshore wind and (hopefully) bright sunshine. However, the skipper must remain alert to the possibility that the depression may track further south, or may be followed by a secondary 'low' that runs up the Channel, either of which events could produce an easterly wind. On the coast of France, the winds are governed by the same factors, but a veer towards north-west is less welcome because many of the anchorages are open to the north.

Sustained easterly winds occur when barometric pressure over the Continent is lower than over the British Isles. There are usually a few days of hazy skies and short, steep waves but the weather can turn nasty if the low pressure decides to track north, as that will often produce thunderstorms. This scenario is particularly inconvenient for a yacht lying in shelter, in an anchorage that is protected from the east but open to the west. The arrival of the thundery cells is likely to be accompanied by heavy rain, squalls and sudden wind shifts. Then, when the skipper is feeling thoroughly disoriented, the low pressure moves off to the north, the wind settles in the west and the anchorage is definitely no longer sheltered. The two occasions on which we were compelled to leave anchorages at night, as mentioned in the Introduction, occurred in just these conditions.

When an anchorage is sheltered by dry land, the degree of protection and comfort will depend upon the nature of the landmass. A low barrier, such as a shingle spit, leaves an anchored yacht exposed to the full force of the wind. However, that force is likely to be fairly steady and there is protection against waves, which would otherwise cause snatch-loading on the anchor. A hill forms a more substantial windbreak but some hills can 'draw down' high level airflow, so that powerful and sustained gusts may be encountered on the downwind side of high ground, particularly where the land follows a regular slope from the peak down to sea level. In the lee of cliffs, it is usually possible to find a patch of glassy, near-windless sea but there are also likely to be gusts hooking over the edge of the land, creating dark, ruffled blotches where they drop on to the water and spread out across its surface. It is advisable to study the anchorage for a while, to identify the behaviour of the gusts. Where they strike the water, an anchored yacht will sheer around, with the anchor chain subjected to intermittent loads in varying directions. Further offshore, the gusts will be superimposed on a steadier, background wind and the forces acting on the anchor will be greater but less variable. Further inshore, there may be puffs of breeze eddying in under the cliffs, causing anchored vessels to swing into shallower water.

A tree-lined shore usually makes for a relaxing anchorage. The vegetation not only forms a rough ground covering, which reduces the surface wind speed, but it also combs out the gusts.

One sometimes reads that an anchorage is 'suitable only for lunch stops in settled weather', or words to that effect, implying that doom threatens anyone who has the temerity to remain overnight. The place being described is often a small bay, offering shelter from only one wind direction. However, if the wind is blowing from that direction and is likely to continue doing so, the anchorage may well be satisfactory. It will be particularly suitable for an overnight stop if there is an easy exit route to open water, just in case the weather does something completely out of character. An anchorage that is protected on three sides might be even better, but only so long as the wind does not come from the open side. It could actually be more risky if there is a significant chance of a wind shift and the exit route is difficult in the dark.

Thermal winds

In fine weather, sea breezes are relevant to anchoring strategy because, although they are rarely very strong, they do cause notable wind shifts. It is conventional to depict sea breezes on diagrams of vertical circulation: warm air rising over the land and cooler air being drawn in from the sea. This is a localised picture but, for a broader view of the effect upon coastal waters, it can be helpful to consider the phenomenon as predominantly horizontal surface airflow, influenced by barometric pressure.

Figure 2 illustrates a common situation at about mid-day in fine weather with minimal cloud cover. (Perhaps there is a light gradient wind from the north but, for the sake of clarity, this has been omitted from the diagram.) Warming has caused a slight reduction in pressure over the land and breezes are being drawn in from seaward but have not managed to climb over the high cliffs of Dorset or to penetrate the Rade de Brest. In the Solent, there is a calm area off Cowes, where the new breezes are blocked by the Isle of Wight. On the opposite side of the Channel, air is being drawn on to the Cotentin Peninsula from both sides. At this stage, the larger Channel Islands may even have their own miniature sea breeze cells, usually creating gentle, fitful puffs that merely confuse the gradient wind.

Figure 3 represents the same day, in the late afternoon, when the breezes have matured and have penetrated further inland. In many areas, they have been influenced by the Coriolis effect and

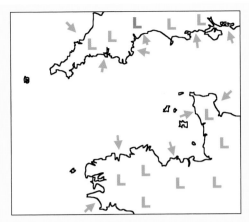

Fig 2 An example of midday sea breezes (L = area of relatively low pressure, caused by the warming of land).

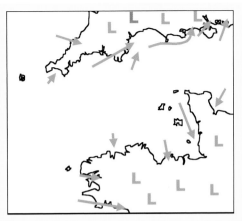

Fig 3 An example of of developed sea breezes (L = area of relatively low pressure, caused by the warming of land).

have veered so that low pressure is on their left. The warming of the continental land mass is also exerting a general pull that tends to draw air in from the west. On the English side of the Channel, a predominantly westerly airflow extends right across the bulge of south Devon, along the Dorset coast to the east of Portland and into the western Solent. In French waters, the powerful sea breeze of southern Brittany is evident as a WNW wind at the southern edge of the diagram, and another strong draught is blowing down the western side of Cotentin. On the northern coast of Brittany, the breeze is less vigorous, possibly because the veering influence is conflicting with the continental pull.

I must emphasise that this illustration does not represent a universal prediction because such breezes are influenced by many variables, including the gradient winds and local variations in cloud cover. For instance, if the day had started with a fresh gradient wind from the north-east, it would probably have strengthened over the Channel Islands and north Brittany as the thermal effects intensified the pressure gradient. I do not aspire to be a meteorologist but all the local winds and directional shifts shown on these diagrams have been observed on several occasions and some of them are routinely predictable.

If a yacht is in an anchorage that is sheltered from the afternoon sea breeze, the skipper's decision on whether to remain overnight will depend upon what is likely to happen when the sea breeze dies. One possibility is that the gradient wind will reassert itself. However, if the weather is fine and a clear sky persists, the land will cool rapidly during the night and this may create a temperature inversion, a shallow layer of cool air, close above the ground, which kills the surface breeze. Temperature inversions can cast a blanket of calm over coastal waters, although they may not extend as far as offshore islands.

Another possibility is a land breeze, caused when the land cools to a temperature lower than that of the sea and induces an offshore airflow that is the reverse of the sea breeze. Land breezes are usually gentle and are often smothered by temperature inversions, but are most likely to be noticed where cooling air collects and flows out of river valleys. If cool air pours down a steep incline it can generate a more vigorous katabatic wind and there are a few coastal anchorages where sloping cliffs produce quite violent katabatic gusts, although their effects are localised.

Most of these nocturnal winds blow off the shore and are therefore unlikely to seriously trouble an anchored yacht. However, if the original gradient wind had been blowing onshore, its resurgence in the early hours of the morning would be inconvenient. This problem typically occurs where an anchorage is sheltered from a westerly sea breeze but is exposed to a gradient wind from north-east or east.

Boltholes

It is always advisable to have a contingency plan, in case a wind shift does make an anchorage untenable. In some areas, the only safe option will be to head for open water and stay there. However, an anchorage may be close to a harbour or to other anchorages that offer shelter from different wind directions. Before settling down for the night in an open bay, one should plan the pilotage for a night departure and, if possible, identify an alternative haven that could serve as a bolthole.

Coastal currents

Where a tidal stream is deflected by a headland, so that it diverges from the coast, this usually induces a rotational motion in the water that is close inshore and downstream of the divergence. Coastal anchorages are typically located behind sheltering headlands or within bays, so many of them are affected by such eddies or counter-currents.

Figure 4 shows a typical situation where an eddy is developing on the downstream side of a headland. This is also the downwind side and two yachts are at anchor. The one that is further from the headland is lying to the wind, in a zone of slack current, but the other is lying to the eddy, with the wind on her quarter. As time passes and the main tidal stream begins to slacken, the eddy will enlarge as shown in Figure 5, possibly reaching the other anchored yacht, and may even extend around the headland, pushing the main stream further offshore. In Figure 6 the tide has turned. Close to the headland, the current is strong and the anchored yacht is again lying with the wind on her quarter. The other yacht is in a weaker current and is generally head to wind, although sheering around her anchor.

Following the next change of tide, there will be a period when the streams are weak and both yachts lie head to wind. In the zone near to the headland, however, the current flows towards the headland for more than half of each tidal cycle – perhaps nine hours out of twelve – and this can

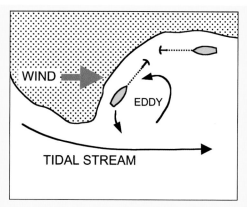

Fig 4 Tidal eddy downstream of a headland.

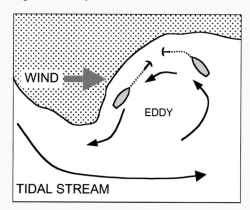

Fig 5 Currents at a headland, just before the turn of the tide.

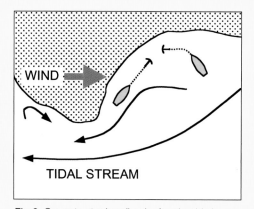

Fig 6 Currents at a headland, after the tide has turned.

affect conditions on board. For instance, the yacht close to the headland is well sheltered, tucked in under the windward shore but if the weather is unsettled, rain may drive under her spray hood and down the hatch. To a skipper who is nervous about the anchor holding, this might seem a minor problem, but coastal cruising should be enjoyable. Choice of anchoring position may influence comfort, particularly for the crewmember sleeping in the leeward quarter berth.

Inshore tidal phenomena are also relevant to passage planning. If a tidal eddy starts to push around the headland, as shown in Figure 5, that provides an opportunity for the yachts to start a windward passage with the very first of a favourable current, before the main stream has turned. In effect, the tide inshore has turned early. In some places, elongated eddies form counter-currents along several miles of coast and it is often possible to make good progress, in a direction contrary to the main tidal stream, by staying close to shore.

When inshore tidal streams interact with waves and swell, they create other effects that are relevant to both anchoring and passage planning. These topics are examined in Chapter 4.

3 Away from the Crowds – in the Solent

The Solent has plenty of room for sailing but its harbours become overcrowded on summer weekends. Diligent organisers of cruiser rallies book their Cowes marina berths several months ahead; yachts race to reach Yarmouth before the 'harbour full' sign goes up; on the Newtown River, closely spaced boats sheer around their anchors, each dancing to its own tune and threatening its neighbour's topsides. This is a microcosm of the English Channel: newcomers are charmed by the harbours but then start to wonder about quieter options, becoming aware of yachts lying peacefully at anchor, in the shelter of wooded shores, their crews sunbathing while the world hurries past. Couples with small children notice that other yachts have brought up close to beaches, which look good for swimming and sandcastles.

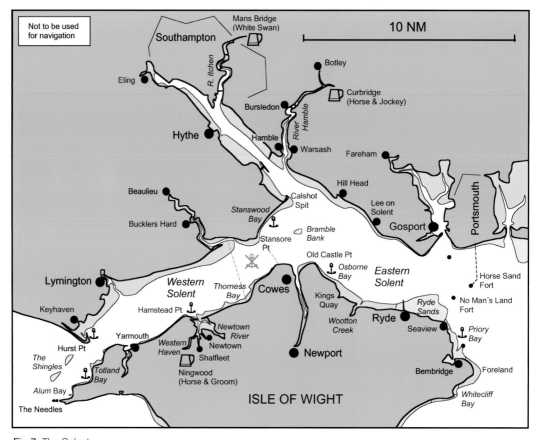

Fig 7 The Solent.

The UKHO Solent Leisure Folio is probably the most useful set of charts for exploring this area. Imray Chart C3 is cheaper and is adequate for the anchorages, although additional large-scale plans are required for some of the inlets.

Although the Solent is protected by the Isle of Wight, certain factors limit the choice of good anchorages. In most areas there are wide, drying foreshores. At some locations, deep water can be found close to dry land but strong currents or wash from shipping traffic cause disturbance. East winds are inconvenient: Lee on Solent offers shelter but the backdrop is suburban, while Thorness Bay looks ideal for easterlies but part of it is within a 'no anchoring' zone. Fortunately, westerly winds are more common.

That leaves us with half a dozen places that are worth describing in detail. The first is at the eastern end of the Isle of Wight, where a vessel that is bound down Channel will find the first coastal anchorage, apart from Dungeness, to offer good shelter from the prevailing winds.

Priory Bay

THE BEACHES OF PRIORY BAY AND SEAGROVE BAY are arguably the best in the Solent area. Yachts often anchor north of St Helen's Fort, near to the tide gauge, while waiting for sufficient rise of tide to enter Bembridge Harbour, but few strangers venture close inshore, because the charts show a quarter-mile spread of drying sands. Nevertheless, local boat owners use these bays for weekend anchorages, bathing and barbecues. New-comers should take some trouble to familiarise themselves with the complex foreshore topography, which will determine their anchoring strategy.

In each bay, sand and shingle form a fairly steep slope close to the HW mark. At the toe of this upper beach, tidal scour and wave action usually create a wide, shallow gully, with a raised bank of sand further offshore. Figure 8 shows the approximate sand levels at the time of our last visit but the banks shift from year to year. An initial approach should be made with a good rise of tide, using the echo sounder to determine the relative levels of the banks and gullies.

For a visiting yacht, there are several anchoring options. First, it is possible to lie in deep water, outside the banks, perhaps moving closer inshore for the high tide period. A move back to deep water must be made in good time, before the boat becomes trapped inshore of the banks. Shoal-draught boats have an advantage during neap tides, when they may be able to anchor in the gullies and yet remain afloat at low water. The bed level of each gully is usually fairly close above chart datum and MLWN is 1.9m.

For boats that can take the ground, the principal hazard is shipping wash, much of it generated by ferry traffic between Portsmouth

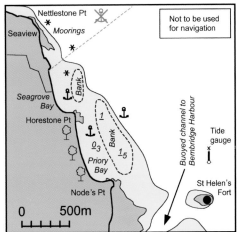

Fig 8 Priory and Seagrove Bays (note that the sand levels change).

Priory Bay at high tide.

and France. If wash arrives just as a yacht is touching down or floating off, she will be bounced on the firm sand. If a yacht is anchored in a gully, however, and if the difference in level between bank and gully is greater than her draught, the bank should uncover, to act as a breakwater, before she touches the bottom. In Priory Bay, some locals beach their boats inshore of the gully, on the relatively steep slope of the upper foreshore. When a boat is taking the ground on a distinct gradient, with her bows pointing uphill, wave action tends to cause a fore-and-aft rocking motion, rather than lifting and dropping the hull. This technique should be used with caution but is often helpful for beaching in less-than-placid conditions.

There are rocks and boulders close to Horestone Point and in the northern part of Seagrove Bay. In the middle of each bay, the sand is usually clear of weed and large stones but one may find the occasional concrete mooring sinker. Seagrove Bay has a dozen or more small boat moorings, so Priory Bay has more swinging room.

In fine weather and west or south-west winds, these anchorages are delightful, with Priory Bay offering slightly better shelter. For swimmers, there is often a bonus as the rising tide flows in over sun-warmed banks to create bathing conditions that are almost cosy. Seaview has several shops and there is a freshwater tap, at a public convenience close to a slipway in the southern part of Seagrove Bay. The nearest bolthole is Bembridge Harbour, although entry is not possible at low water.

Further south and just around the corner of the island, Whitecliff Bay is sheltered from north-west winds. The bold chalk cliff provides some protection from the west, but much of the bay is filled with sand and a yacht that is tucked in behind the cliff will be in shallow water. There is often some swell from the south-west.

Osborne Bay

THIS BAY IS GENERALLY USED AS A LUNCH STOP or to await a fair tide, rather than as an overnight anchorage. It has deep water and provides good shelter from south-west winds, although waves from the western Solent can find their way around Old Castle Point to cause rolling, particularly when the tide is running to the west. There are some groups of rocks on the foreshore. Further out, the holding appears to be reliable, on muddy gravel.

It is widely assumed that the public enjoys access to all British beaches below the high water mark, as the foreshore generally belongs to the Crown Estate. Unfortunately, a few coastal landowners also own their foreshores and in some places, including Osborne, landing on the beach is prohibited. However, if the crew demand entertainment, why not launch the tender and make a high water excursion to Kings Quay Creek, a mile to the south? This enchanting inlet is a nature reserve but the waterway is accessible by boat. To preserve the tranquillity, please use oars rather than outboard motor. The entrance is partly concealed between overlapping shingle spits and is not obvious from offshore. Inside the spits, a narrow channel winds through the saltings, past the stumps of ancient timber jetties and below overhanging trees, leading to a derelict sluice and a quiet mere where wildfowl cruise between the reed beds.

A water skiing area lies offshore and Osborne Bay is popular with corporate entertainment charter boats, yet Kings Quay feels far away from all the crowds.

Stanswood Bay

LESS POPULAR THAN OSBORNE BAY, Stanswood is a better anchorage if the wind veers to west or north-west. It is also a good spot for awaiting a fair tide, whether one is bound westward or heading up Southampton Water.

This is another place where landing is prohibited on part of the beach, in this case the privately owned middle third of the foreshore (the area is marked by fences and notices). However, there are public beaches at both ends of the bay. Towards Calshot, the foreshore becomes wider and the bay shallower, so yachts must anchor well out if they are not to ground at low water. Close to Stansore Point there is deep water close to the land but westerly winds send waves around the point. During the east-going flood, an eddy develops to the east of the point, so vessels anchored here spend about three quarters of each tidal cycle in a stream flowing south-west.

Stanswood harbours one unwelcome secret. Some patches of the seabed consist of a thin covering of sand overlying hard clay. The upper few centimetres of the clay are weathered and softened, so that the combination has the properties of greased rock. We do not allow this to deter us from anchoring but it is essential to pull the anchor firmly into the bottom, so that the point becomes properly embedded and is not merely resting in the shallow layer of sand.

There is a small café among the Calshot beach huts and a freshwater tap at the nearby public conveniences.

Hamstead Point

THE WESTERN SOLENT IS OFTEN A RATHER DRAUGHTY PLACE, experiencing a high proportion of south-westerly winds that whistle straight up the fairway. The island shore offers shelter from south-east winds but, when a south-easterly is associated with an approaching depression, it is often expected to veer towards south-west and strengthen. If the depression holds off, the weather may be fine but this is quite likely to generate a sea breeze, again from the south-west. In these conditions, one of the few geographical features to offer useful protection is Hamstead Point, immediately west of the Newtown River. The protection is not generous, and becomes non-existent if the wind veers to the west, but many yachts use this anchorage as an alternative to Newtown if the latter is crowded.

Close to the point, on most tides, there are anchoring depths within a few metres of the steep shingle beach. Currents are strong, so swimmers should take care. In general, the holding is good but we have encountered patches of thick, loose weed in shallower water, near to the river mouth and south of its entrance channel, where tidal streams are too weak to scour the bottom.

On the shore, footpaths connect the visitor to the island's walking network, including a path to Yarmouth and some lovely strolls through meadowland. The nearest shop is the Post Office store at Shalfleet, reached by a one-mile dinghy trip to Shalfleet Quay and a half-mile walk. There is a freshwater tap about 200m inland of Newtown Quay, at the end of a boardwalk that leads over the marshes towards the old Newtown village.

Hurst

HURST SPIT IS A LONG, LOW, SHINGLE BARRIER between the Solent and the open waters of the Channel. It extends from the mainland for more than a mile, to Hurst Point, and then hooks back to the entrance of Keyhaven Lake. The anchorage, north of the point, is a popular Saturday night stop for weekenders but also makes an excellent departure point for a Channel cruise. We have begun several holidays by riding the last of the ebb down the western Solent and anchoring behind the spit for a few hours' rest before the next fair tide pushes us towards the West Country or France. This is the transition between inshore and offshore: a chance to check tidal predictions and the weather forecast, stow loose gear and make the boat snug for open water. Waves can be heard breaking on the seaward side of the spit and there is a pleasant sensation of 'here we go'.

The spit and the Hampshire shore provide shelter from winds between south-west and north, while the Isle of Wight limits the fetch from south and south-east, so the anchorage is only really exposed to east and north-east. The bottom is mainly sand or shingle, with depths between 1m and 2m over a fairly wide area but shallower to the north and dropping off sharply to the 60m-deep scour hole in Hurst Narrows. The ebb stream flows through the anchorage in a southerly direction. As the flood tide pours into the Solent through the Narrows, an eddy develops behind the spit and again creates a southerly current in the outer part of the anchorage.

If unpromising weather delays further progress, there are several sources of entertainment. On the end of the spit, Hurst Castle is maintained by English Heritage and is open to summer visitors. Henry VIII commissioned the central tower with its small, semicircular bastions and much of the original structure is preserved but the dominant features are now the long Victorian wing batteries that housed huge, rifled muzzle-loading guns, two of which have been refurbished and remounted. The end of the spit feels more like an island than a peninsula and the seventeenth-century garrison was sufficiently isolated to be able to devote its energies to smuggling. The castle was never called upon to resist a sea-borne invasion but the raised drawbridge was sufficient to foil a raid by customs officers.

Most visitors to the castle from the mainland now arrive on the Keyhaven ferry rather than by trudging along the shingle. In the evening, when they have departed, the only remaining humans are a few anglers and the crews of anchored yachts. This is a fine place for a barbecue.

The entrance to Keyhaven Lake is very shallow (about 0.5m at LAT) but there is an anchorage in a slightly deeper pool, close inside the northern extremity of the spit and sheltered from the east. This has room for only a few boats and is silting up from the south as the spit gradually extends towards the north. The channel winds through the saltings to Keyhaven, where there is no shop but the Gun Inn is a good venue for lunch or dinner and there is a freshwater tap at the public conveniences.

Totland Bay

STRICTLY SPEAKING, THIS BAY IS OUTSIDE THE SOLENT but it belongs to the Solent cruising area and enables this chapter to include one anchorage that is sheltered from the east. Like Hurst, Totland serves as a pleasant weekend retreat, or as a daytime destination in fine weather, when boats sluice out through Hurst Narrows with the ebb, lie off the beach and then return home on the flood. Like Hurst, it may also serve as a good passage anchorage. Our most recent Channel crossing from France was a fast reach in a stiff east wind, on a wonderful day of bright sun, blue sky and perfect visibility. We swept in around the Needles in the early evening, feeling peckish, just as the tide was turning to the west. Reaching Yarmouth would have entailed a long slog against the strengthening current and it seemed a shame to end such a splendid sail by starting the engine. There was just enough wind to tack into Totland Bay to anchor west of the pier, where the breeze was hardly ruffling the flat water. It was September and only two people were eating in the restaurant that overlooks the bay. We dined at our cockpit table, warmed by the setting sun.

Totland offers shelter from south and east and the middle of the bay is free of hazards. Within the bay, tidal streams are weak, despite the powerful currents in the Needles Channel. Close to the pier, the bottom is sand and shelves gently, with depths of 2m within about 100m of the beach. A yacht that is anchored 200m out should have adequate swinging room in the event of a wind shift. To the north, the rocks of Warden Ledge extend nearly half a mile from the shore. Along the southern side of the bay, charts show the rocks extending less than 100m from the foot of the cliffs but we have observed lumps that appeared to lie further out. It is possible that these were loose boulders from the crumbly cliffs, that had been moved across the shallow seabed by wave action, so I am inclined to keep well clear of this shoreline.

Totland is open to westerly winds and Channel swell, although the latter may be suppressed by the west-going ebb stream and become more noticeable during the flood. The obvious bolthole is the anchorage at Hurst. There is a freshwater tap near to the pier and a few shops in the village, which is reached via a short, steep path.

The adjacent Alum Bay forms a slightly deeper indentation and looks as if it should be slightly better protected by the island. It certainly has more picturesque, multi-coloured cliffs but those cliffs can cause strong gusts. There are also some shallow and drying rocks within the anchoring area.

UP-RIVER OPTIONS

Let's imagine that the weather has turned blustery from the south, and prevents immediate exploration of the Dorset coast. Having tried the Solent's anchorages, the crew are looking for some more entertainment. How about a trip into the jungle? For the following expeditions, it is useful to carry Ordnance Survey maps on a scale of 1:25,000.

The Upper Hamble

SOME JUNGLE: A JUNGLE OF MASTS? Readers will be familiar with the Hamble's reputation as a boat park but half the tidal river lies upstream of the bridges of Bursledon and is a world away from the high-intensity water sports of the lower estuary. If the Lower Hamble is all leisure industry, the Upper Hamble is just leisure.

At Bursledon, the lowest bridge clearance is 4m at MHWS, so most visitors who wish to penetrate to the real head of navigation will leave the parent yacht in one of the marinas or on a visitors' mooring, before heading inland by tender. The tide rushes under the bridges, past rows of new powerboats and the second-hand chandlery store on its concrete lighter, then the rumble of the M27 falls astern and the river becomes thoroughly rural. The Manor Farm Country Park lies to port and somewhere below the water, largely buried in the mud, are the bones of Henry VIII's great warship, the *Henry Grace à Dieu*. This reach is a popular fishing ground: herons wade along in the shallows, kingfishers flash low over the surface and human anglers anchor in midstream. They do not fear being run down by river traffic because there is hardly any. Along the banks, some of the minor creeks make perfect picnic spots.

The estuary splits two miles upstream of Bursledon, with the Curbridge arm diverging to the east. The main river leads to Botley, winding through water meadows and narrowing to little more than a leafy, suburban ditch before reaching the tidal limit at the main road, in a shallow pool overlooked by the old Botley Mill. At the southern limit of the built-up

Upstream of the bridges at Bursledon, the River Hamble is a leafy backwater.

area, where the tributary of Pudbrook Lake joins the river, there is a small quay that has been restored by the local authority. This serves as a landing point for access to the town. Near to the quay, the bed of the river is about 3m above chart datum.

Most up-river explorers choose to follow the Curbridge arm, which snakes through reed beds and into the woods. This resembles a proper jungle and one would hardly be surprised to meet Humphrey Bogart and Katharine Hepburn wading around a bend, pulling the *African Queen* behind them. On our most recent expedition to these parts, we encountered a pair of swans which, like us, were floating their way upstream with the rising tide. The gravel bed rises quite steeply and we saw no point in getting out to push. They were equally reluctant to stand up and walk. We all seemed to be heading for lunch and, half a mile from the confluence with the main river, our dinghy finally nudged alongside the landing stage at the Horse and Jockey pub. The swans hung around in the river, looking expectant and presumably hoping for surplus sandwiches.

In 1932, a less common marine animal arrived at Curbridge by mistake. An 11-foot narwhal had taken a wrong turning and became stranded in a shallow pool. Its timing was all wrong: in the twenty-first century, it would have become a celebrity, featured on the TV news, surrounded by rescuers and shepherded back to the sea. In 1932, things were different: a beast was a beast and a strange beast was potentially profitable. The poor narwhal was hauled ashore, shot and put on show to the public, who flocked to see it at tuppence a peek.

At the Horse and Jockey's landing stage, according to my estimate, the bed of the river is approximately 3.6m above chart datum. MHWN is only 3.8m but MHWS is 4.6m, so this voyage is best undertaken at spring tides. Fortunately, in the Solent area, spring tides have high water at about mid-day, which is convenient for pub lunches.

Up the Itchen

THIS IS ANOTHER ESTUARY OF TWO HALVES. The banks of the downstream half used to resemble Thames docklands and their redevelopment has followed a similar pattern, with most shipping traffic displaced to container ports, marinas in the old dock basins, offices and up-market housing on the quays. As on the Thames, however, a quieter environment can be found upstream of the low bridges. There is also an opportunity to perform a public service.

Mooring sites for visiting yachts include Ocean Village, Shamrock Quay or Kemps' marina. It is also possible to anchor over the edge of the mudflats, downstream of Northam Bridge, but there are several unmarked wrecks in this area. A low-masted vessel or motorboat could travel further upstream but the crew must embark in the tender for a voyage to the absolute limit of navigation.

Above Northam Bridge, the character of the river changes and the back gardens of houses lead down to the water, sprouting pontoons and slipways. Beyond Cobden Bridge, the Riverside Park has a permanent, miniature railway track on which model engineers demonstrate their creations, which puff through the bushes in clouds of steam. The last half-mile of the tidal estuary is lined by reed beds and ends abruptly in a tree-lined pool at Woodmill. This was once the site of Woodmill Lock and the start of the 10-mile Itchen Navigation, which led to Winchester.

The lock no longer exists but a short portage will take the dinghy across the road, where it can be re-launched on clear, fresh water that has come from the chalk aquifer and watercress beds of northern Hampshire. It flows swiftly but there is only about another half-mile to go, under Mans Bridge, which was the Itchen's lowest medieval crossing point, and on to the terrace of the White Swan. It will probably be necessary to moor the dinghy to a potted plant because the pub's management does not expect many visiting boats.

It would be possible to cover the last half-mile via the riverside path, but that would miss the whole point of the expedition. An elderly gentleman summed it up perfectly as we rowed past him. He was walking slowly, accompanied by his wife and their dogs, but he waved his stick and smiled broadly. 'I am glad', he said, 'That someone is taking the trouble to maintain the right of navigation!'

On the canalised Itchen, between Woodmill and Winchester, an 1802 Act of Parliament established the right of public navigation. Trade on the waterway ceased in 1869 and part of the canal, which diverges from the river upstream of Mans Bridge, has become an overgrown ditch where the shortsighted designers of the M27 decided to culvert it through the motorway embankment. However, the right of navigation still exists; the shares of the Navigation Company have apparently been lost and the Act has never been repealed.

We have already come across some Solent beaches from which the public are excluded. There has, as yet, been no suggestion of restricting access to the non-tidal part of the Itchen but it seems a good idea to exercise one's rights from time to time, in case anybody should attempt to extinguish them.

Western Haven

FOR A FINAL UP-RIVER JOURNEY before we leave the Solent, let's assume that we have anchored in the Newtown River but there appear to be large numbers of heavily laden tenders heading for the New Inn at Shalfleet, so we should like to find a quieter alternative. If we start by following the crowd but then ignore Shalfleet Lake and bear to starboard, this course leads into Western Haven. It is such a marvellously tranquil creek that I feel hesitant about recommending it to potential visitors, but I doubt whether a few tenders will cause harm.

The channel winds for a mile between wooded shores and grassy banks that always seem to be covered in wild flowers, before reaching a bridge where the Hamstead Track crosses the waterway. Dinghies can pass under the narrow arch and continue for a very shallow quarter-mile to where the tidal water peters out in a meadow. However, sailors who are looking for lunch should moor their boats close to the bridge, walk southward along the track for about 500m, then turn right along the main road for another 200m (sorry about the traffic on this bit), to reach the Horse and Groom at Ningwood. At the bridge, the water is fairly shallow and there is an obvious risk of being left high and dry by the retreating tide, so it is best to time this trip carefully. If boats come upstream with the flood, the double high tide should allow visitors at least a couple of hours before the bathwater starts to run out.

4 Coastal Waves

Where this book describes partly sheltered anchorages, a significant proportion of the text is devoted to waves. Readers who usually moor in marinas may conclude that I am paranoid about waves and swell but those who are accustomed to wilder shores will be much more understanding. When we are contemplating a visit to an anchorage, there are three principal considerations:

1   What will be the wind direction?
2   Will the anchorage be affected by waves or swell?
3   What is the best pilotage plan for entry and exit?

Unless our answers to questions 1 and 2 are satisfactory, question 3 is probably irrelevant. Winds and wind shifts have been examined earlier. This chapter looks at some of the complexities of wave action.

In coastal waters, the behaviour of waves is influenced by shoals and by currents, with implications for both comfort and safety. Waves are deflected into sheltered bays, low swell becomes unexpectedly steeper and yachts that cruise between the more exciting anchorages may spend a proportion of their time in the vicinity of tidal overfalls. Even if an anchorage is placid, rough water in the approaches is unwelcome because it is difficult to think objectively and keep a cool head when foam is sluicing over the pilotage marks and both chart table and cockpit are lurching violently.

On the other hand, some of the factors that create steep waves in one location will induce relatively smooth conditions in another. This is because virtually all wave energy comes from the wind. Shoals and currents influence the waves but do not, generally, add to their energy. Therefore, if wave energy becomes concentrated in one place, an adjoining area may actually become calmer. Areas of rougher water can often be avoided, if we are able to anticipate the likely wave patterns.

Some wave theory

Much of the wave behaviour discussed in this chapter is associated with the velocity of waves, which is governed by the wavelength (the distance between successive wave crests) and the depth of water. In very deep water, the velocity of waves is simply proportional to the square root of their wavelength, so that longer waves travel faster. The actual formula is:

Wave velocity (in knots) = 2.48 x square root of wavelength (in metres)

In relatively shallow water, wave velocity is reduced; this effect becomes noticeable where the depth is less than about half the wavelength.

Wave refraction caused by shoal water

When waves approach a coast and 'feel the bottom', their velocity is progressively reduced and their wavelength becomes shorter. If the waves are approaching the coast obliquely, those close to the shore are affected first, causing the crests to turn until they are roughly parallel with the shore, a phenomenon known as wave refraction. Where the coastline and the underwater contours are convex in shape (eg at a headland where the seabed shelves up gradually, from deeper water), refraction may bend the wave pattern around the headland and into the 'sheltered' area on the far side: see Figure 9.

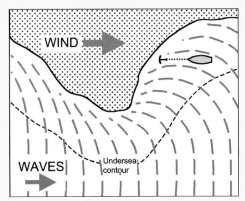

Fig 9 Wave refraction at a headland, caused by shoaling water.

In this diagram, the anchored yacht is sheltered from the wind but is more or less beam-on to the waves. The crew will be cursing: few cruising experiences are more tiresome than rolling at anchor, with crockery rattling, locker doors creaking and everyone trying to brace themselves against the motion.

Wave diffraction

If a headland or breakwater is steep-sided and surrounded by uniformly deep water, rather than a shelving seabed, waves will not refract around it. However, a process known as diffraction may cause a similar effect, shown in Figure 10. As each wave passes the end of the breakwater, the rise

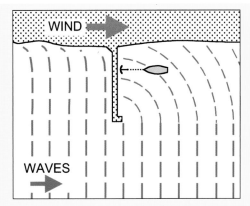

Fig 10 Wave diffraction at a breakwater.

and fall of the sea generates a new wave, which radiates into the area behind the wall. These diffracted waves are smaller than refracted waves but can be equally irritating for the crew of a vessel that is supposedly lying in shelter.

Effective protection

Refraction and diffraction are most noticeable where the seabed has a smooth profile, so that the waves are redirected without losing their regularity. If the seabed is undulating, waves are refracted in several different directions; the resulting mixture of waves, criss-crossing within an anchorage, may produce an agitated movement but is less likely to induce rhythmic rolling and bad language. Similarly, a broken chain of rocks or islands, with narrow gaps, will often suppress waves more effectively than a solid breakwater, because diffraction occurs at each of the gaps and the separate wave systems interfere with one another. If a bay is deeply indented, so that waves have to turn through more than 90° in order to enter, that will make a good anchorage. It will be even better if the protecting headlands are ragged, with detached islands, rocks and submerged banks to break up the wave pattern.

Making the best of a rolling anchorage

If an anchorage is affected by wave action, there are several possible remedies (quite apart from the obvious one of leaving for somewhere else). In

Figure 9, the yacht would ride more easily if a kedge anchor were deployed to hold her stern towards the waves, so that her motion was one of pitching rather than rolling. On the other hand, if a current were flowing through the anchorage towards the headland, as in Figure 4 (page 8), that could hold her stern to the waves and achieve the same result. Steadying canvas might help: perhaps a tightly sheeted mizzen, a reefed mainsail or even a jib hoisted on the backstay and sheeted forward.

Each of these techniques has drawbacks. Kedging is positively antisocial in a crowded anchorage, where cables become crossed. The eddy current only flows towards the headland for part of the tidal cycle (and the benefit of reduced rolling may have to be balanced against the disadvantage of wind and rain down the hatch). Steadying canvas seems to work better on some boats than on others.

If all else fails, we deploy our flopper stopper (Figure 11). This device is suspended underwater from the end of the boom, which is swung outboard and secured forward by a preventer. The flopper stopper sinks freely on each downward roll of the boom and then resists the upward roll. It cannot prevent rolling completely because some movement is necessary before it creates resistance, but it has the effect of damping the motion, breaking the rhythm and making life on board much more comfortable.

Various types of flopper stopper have been invented, including milk crates with flap valves in the bottom. Ours was developed from the design published by Eric Hiscock in his book *Cruising Under Sail*. It is a triangular board, weighted at one corner and suspended from a three-part bridle. On the downward roll, the bridle slackens and the weighted corner pulls the board down, edge first. On the return roll, the bridle snatches taut so that the board becomes horizontal and resists the upward force.

During the 'snatch', there is a slight delay. Before the board becomes horizontal, the boom must pull the bridle upward by a distance equal to the width of the board (measured from the weighted corner to the opposite side). In the original design, the board was an equilateral triangle. To minimise the delay in each snatch, we have reduced the width of the board, while maintaining the same area, by making it as an isosceles triangle with the weight at the obtuse angle.

Wave refraction caused by currents

When waves move against a current, it reduces their velocity over the ground. If the current is flowing past an area of slack water, waves that reach the boundary between the current and the slack water tend to move forward faster. This has the effect of swinging the wave crests back into the current: see Figure 12. Only a fraction of the wave energy propagates into the slack water, so the current acts as a liquid breakwater. Where a

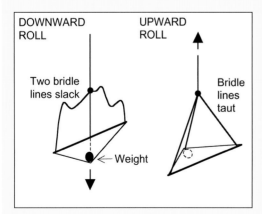

Fig 11 A flopper stopper in action.

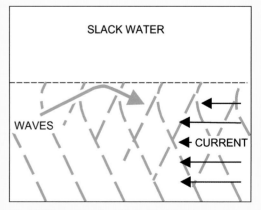

Fig 12 Wave refraction at a boundary between an adverse current and slack water.

current flows across the mouth of a bay in a direction that is generally contrary to the waves, this type of refraction will often make the bay calmer. However, the effect is reversed when the current changes direction.

Some more wave theory

The velocity of a wave is the velocity of its crest but the energy in a wave system only moves at half the velocity of the wave crests. This phenomenon can be verified by carefully watching a small group of waves, such as the spreading, circular group that is created when a stone is dropped into water. As the group moves across the surface, individual waves move faster than the group, appearing at the rear of the group and overtaking it until they fade away at the front edge. (For a mechanical analogy, consider a group of cylindrical rollers, resting on the ground and supporting a moving load. The group of rollers moves forward at half the velocity of the load, which is in contact with the top of each roller.)

In the open sea, the visible waves are created by a combination of several wave trains (which are, in effect, elongated wave groups), each with a different wavelength. Ripples ride on short waves that are, in their turn, superimposed on longer waves, etc. This mix of wavelengths is known as the wave spectrum.

Overfalls

Water likes to flow downhill. In the sea, shoals baulk the tide so that the current is relatively weak on the upstream side of a shoal, stronger where it falls over the edge of the shoal and then weaker downstream. The downward drop across the shoal is usually imperceptible, although there are a few places, such as narrow gaps within reefs, where a big spring tide can create a noticeable 'step' in the sea's surface.

If the open sea is calm, there may be turbulence downstream of a shoal, possibly accompanied by some foam and noise, but any waves created by the current are relatively small. However, if wind-driven waves are rolling upstream and enter the faster patch of adverse current, their wave energy becomes concentrated, to produce much rougher conditions. As each wave meets the stronger current, its velocity over the ground is reduced and the following wave catches up a little. This shortens the wavelength and therefore causes a further reduction in wave velocity, compounding the compression of the wave pattern. As noted above, the wave energy moves at only half the wave velocity, so a comparatively modest increase in the current may be sufficient to bring the wave energy to a complete stop. In fact, it can be shown mathematically that waves moving from slack water on to an adverse current are stopped by a current velocity equal to one quarter of the wave velocity.

When waves are 'stopped', it is the movement of wave energy that is halted. The foreshortened waves continue to move forward slowly but fade away where they meet the strongest current, usually over the shallowest part of the shoal or over its downstream edge: see Figure 13. When

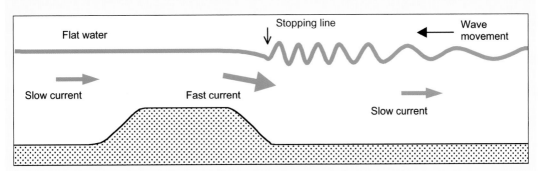

Fig 13 Overfalls, with short waves being completely stopped by an increase in adverse current.

viewed from upstream, the stopping line appears as an abrupt line of steep wave faces, rising and falling. It is often described, incorrectly, as a line of 'standing waves'.

Under open-sea conditions, where the wave spectrum normally includes several wavelengths, a localised increase in adverse current will stop only the shorter waves. As these approach the stopping line, they become much steeper and may break. The longer waves, on the other hand, become foreshortened but continue upstream, over the shoal, until they reach a weaker current and flatten out again. Immediately upstream of the stopping line, these waves appear unnaturally smooth because the shorter waves have been eliminated.

Overfalls can be useful in pilotage because they help to indicate the position of the shoal. There is usually a shallow area immediately upstream of a stopping line. Conversely, if a shoal is shown on a chart, we can expect to find overfalls downstream of it, particularly when the current and the waves are in opposition. It may be possible to avoid the rough water by steering upstream of the shoal, although this entails an obvious risk of being swept over the shoal if there is a failure of wind or motor power.

Waves can also be foreshortened in deep water, if an adverse current is intensified by a constriction, such as a narrow gully, or by a headland, even if there is no shoal. Where there is no variation in depth, the current velocity changes gradually, so that there is no distinct stopping line and the roughest water may occur some distance downstream of the constriction, where the approaching waves first encounter the tongue of stronger current.

Upstream of an overfall, the wave-stopping effect creates relatively calm conditions. On an estuary, particularly if it has a narrow entrance, the ebb tide may appear to sweep out the incoming waves because they are stopped at the river mouth, where they meet the outgoing current. However, this is another kind of liquid breakwater that disappears when the current reverses.

Wind against tide

It is generally recognised that 'wind against tide' causes rough water but inexperienced sailors are often surprised by the degree of violence. When a current flows to windward, it is evident that there must be an increase in apparent wind strength, yet that seems inadequate to explain the dramatic increase in wave activity. In fact, much of the roughness is induced by the process of wave refraction and by overfalls. When refraction swings wave crests into a tongue of adverse current, the wave energy becomes concentrated in the current. Where the speed of the current changes, that concentration is exaggerated by the wave-stopping effect. If these processes are properly understood, it should be possible to plot a course around the areas of unpleasantness.

Swell

When we refer to 'wind against tide', we should really use the term 'waves against tide'. Even under windless conditions, overfalls and wave refraction occur where the movement of swell waves is contrary to a tidal stream. In the English Channel, Atlantic swell from the west is noticeable on most days of the year and many areas of overfalls are at their worst with west-flowing currents.

Waves with tide

In certain places, patches of choppy water are created when waves and currents are moving in the same general direction. If waves are riding on a current that suddenly loses velocity, or changes direction, the effect is much as if those waves had encountered an adverse current. There are some differences, because the waves are foreshortened but not stopped completely, and this type of overfall is usually more random and chaotic than the wave-versus-tide variety. Typically, there are hollow, leaping crests with less force and more froth. The phenomenon can often be observed where waves are riding on a favourable current and then propagate into slack water.

Poole Bay to Bolt Head

5

For cruising yachts, this stretch of coast is Britain's soft south. The weather is dryer than in the far west and the Atlantic swell has lost some of its vigour during its passage up the Channel. Off-lying rocks are infrequent and, for many of the bays and coves, the pilotage amounts to little more than 'turn inshore and drop anchor'. The principal safety considerations are weather and waves, which is why Chapters 2 and 4 explored those subjects in detail. Hardly any of the anchorages provide good shelter from southerly winds and there are several notable tide races.

The first area of interest is the Isle of Purbeck. This peninsula owes its insular title to historical inaccessibility: visitors from up-country were said to have come on to the 'island' when they had skirted the marshes around Poole Harbour and crossed the River Frome at Wareham. It still has navigable water on three sides, with sheltered anchorages to suit most wind directions and scenery to suit most tastes: elegantly sculpted bays, contorted cliffs and some very quiet backwaters. Poole is the nearest major town but the town quay can be risky – yachts have been damaged while lying alongside – and the adjacent marina has fairly high charges. If Mary and I find ourselves spending a few days in this area, whether waiting for a change of wind or simply because we like it, we usually avoid Poole and do our shopping in the towns and villages on the other side of Poole Harbour, either at Wareham or in Purbeck.

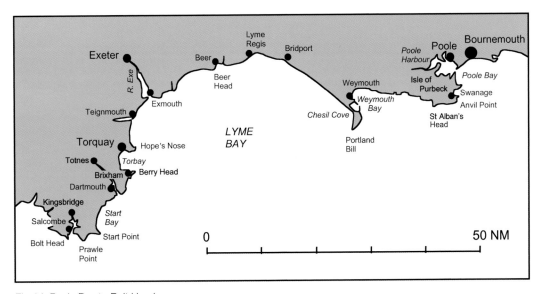

Fig 14 Poole Bay to Bolt Head.

Studland Bay

AT WEEKENDS, STUDLAND IS POOLE'S PLAYGROUND, full of anchored boats, ski boats and hire boats. At other times it is an excellent anchorage, with plenty of room and few hazards. There is good protection from winds between south and NNW, although a prolonged blow from due south will send a swell around Handfast Point's Old Harry Rocks and into the anchorage. Afternoon sea breezes often blow over Purbeck and out of the bay; a NE gradient wind might reassert itself after dark but the northern shore of Poole Bay limits the wave fetch. See Figure 15.

The bay is shallow; best depths are in the southern half but deep-draught yachts may have to anchor a quarter-mile from the beach. Apart from some foul ground near to Handfast Point and the small, drying lump of the Redend Rocks, close to the western shore, the seabed is gently undulating sand. There are thin patches of growing weed but loose weed sometimes collects in the slightly deeper areas. We have never experienced inadequate holding but some boats' crews seem to dangle their anchors vaguely on the bottom and later find that they are only anchored to the loose weed. Check that the hook is dug in!

Studland village has a well-stocked Post Office store and fresh water is available at the head of the track that leads up from the beach. For exercise, a footpath leads on to Ballard Down, from where there are fine views across Poole Harbour and Swanage Bay. For recovery after exercise, the garden of the Bankes Arms overlooks the anchorage.

Swanage Bay

SWANAGE WAS AN INDUSTRIAL TOWN that became a kiss-me-quick holiday resort and is now rediscovering its earlier history. Not at all 'yachty', it is nevertheless a very convenient passage anchorage, only 55 miles from Alderney and a good jumping-off point for a long leg to the West Country.

The bay is sheltered from any wind with west in it although there is often more swell than at Studland. While the tide in the Channel is flowing east, an eddy develops in the bay and spills out past Peveril Point, so that the stream here flows to the south for most of the tidal cycle. A small but potentially nasty overfall is formed where the current crosses the underwater extension of the point and meets the waves or swell that are usually coming in from the Channel. Keeping outside the Peveril Ledge buoy usually avoids the worst of the broken water. The normal anchorage is west of the pier and outside the local moorings, where the bottom is mainly sand with some weed. The mooring area is foul with old gear. At neaps there is sufficient depth for shoal-draught yachts to lie inshore of the moorings but do not make our mistake of arriving on the day of the town regatta and anchoring in the rowing course! Fortunately, everyone was very friendly; we moved a few boatlengths offshore and were well placed for a grandstand view of the evening fireworks.

The main pier is private but it is possible to land by dinghy at a rough slipway (awkward in swell) or on the beach, close to the old, short stone pier. The sailing club is friendly and the town has a good range of shops, a freshwater tap close to the stone pier, and several chippies.

To the east of the pier and an obtrusive modern housing development, the pace of life slows down. Clustered around the lifeboat station is the last remnant of the original fishing village, complete with homemade landing stages. The encircling arms of Peveril Point and Handfast Point gave the bay such good protection from the prevailing winds that no harbour was ever built, and yet Swanage became quite a busy port, prospering from a healthy trade in stone. Much of this came from underground workings within the limestone strata in the hill between the town and the sea, and was stacked all along the shoreline to await shipment. Old trolley rails are still set into the sea wall. The eastern extremities of the strata outcrop at Peveril Point and one vein also appears in the cliffs between Anvil Point and St Alban's Head. Here, extraction was via galleries in the cliff face and some of the stone was lowered directly into boats. The galleries remain, including the so-called 'Tilly Whin Caves', and can be inspected by hugging the shoreline. A hundred metres off may feel close, but just imagine floating right alongside the rock face while kerbstones, flagstones and lintels were lowered from above!

POOLE HARBOUR

Before we press on towards the west, Poole Harbour invites us to make another inland expedition. It will be particularly alluring if the wind persists in blowing from the south-westerly quarter, making a lee shore of almost everything between Anvil Point and the Exe. We might also be tempted by the intriguing complexities of the shallow channels and by the prospect of a night in placid water, with Canada geese begging at our cockpit. Those shallow channels deter some owners of deep-keeled boats but the secret is to enter with the first flood, turn into the designated 'quiet area' south-west of Brownsea Island, and select an anchorage before second high water and the short, rapid ebb.

Up to Wytch Passage

POOLE'S TRADITIONAL ANCHORAGES for south-west winds are off Goathorn, Cleavel and Shipstal Points. At the first two, the zones with the best shelter, close to the shore, are partly obstructed by moorings. Elsewhere, anchored craft are exposed to gusts that pour down off the hillsides and funnel out of the tributary bays. I have memories of spending one fierce night in the reach between Cleavel and Goathorn, with an inflatable dinghy flying from our pushpit like a bulbous kite. In unsettled weather, Shipstal is more restful because the mainland lies to the west and north, saltings provide protection from the south-west, and islands give shelter from the east. Stakes mark the channel as far as Round Island, where beacons warn of a cable crossing. Depths are generally between 0.5m and 1.5m, but MLWN is 1.2m, so there is enough water for most yachts to lie afloat at neaps.

It is possible to go ashore at Shipstal Point but there is another, much less well known landing place further upstream, which can be reached by dinghy. From Round Island, Wych Lake extends deep into the heathland. Saltings fringe the waterway and there are a few rough sticks marking the narrow channel, but they provide incomplete guidance and anyone attempting this trip in a boat larger than a small dinghy would need a

Shipstal Point, in Poole Harbour, looking across the anchorage to Long Island. *Photo: Mary Endean*

sounding pole to find the best water. After passing under a low power cable, one comes at last to Wytch Passage. This was once a loading point for minerals (mainly clay) that were excavated locally, but it also functioned as the 'port' for Corfe Castle and there is a slightly obscure public footpath that still leads towards that town from the water's edge. Only one building remains: a thatched cottage known as 'Passage House', which originally served as the harbour office. Nowadays, its main connection with the sea is that its living room floods during very high tides.

At this point, the channel bed and the mud banks dry by about 0.5m and 1.7m respectively. MHWS is only 2.0m but Poole's double high tides permit a fairly leisurely exploration. Further upstream, there is a wide, shallow mere and then the navigable water ends in a narrow rivulet, which disappears into the reeds. Aquatic wildlife is abundant but, when we visited, the most unusual species present was a traditional working boat: a genuine gun punt, complete with closed rowlocks on outriggers, a long cockpit for lying down and the single gun port forward. It seemed to be a well-protected species, supported above flood level on a grid of scaffold poles and maintained in good order. We were told that it was used very infrequently, which presumably accounted for the apparent nonchalance of the wildfowl.

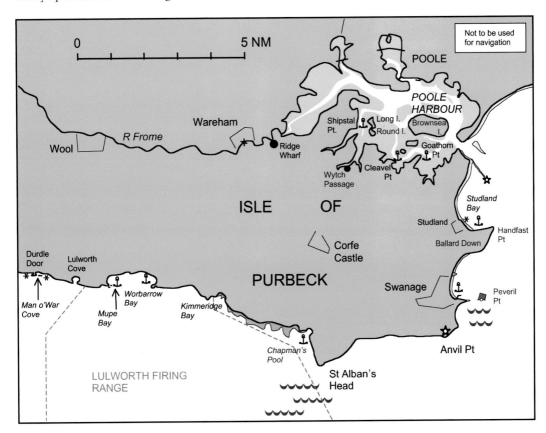

SOUTH PURBECK

West of St Alban's Head, the coast is comprised of relatively young, soft rocks that have eroded into dramatic shapes. The anchorages are all open to the south but some of them offer a degree of shelter from south-west or south-east. To approach this area from the east, it is usual either to make a long detour around the St Alban's Race or to try a short cut through the sometimes-calmer 'inshore passage', close to the land. In my experience this strip of relatively calm water is fairly dependable when the tide is flowing east but is likely to be non-existent if a west-going tide meets a stiff wind or an incoming swell, when steep waves can extend right in to the boulders of the headland. The passage may widen during the later phase of the ebb, when an eddy flows down the west side of St Alban's Head and starts to push the main stream away from the shore.

Immediately west of St Alban's, Chapman's Pool nestles under the dark, oil-bearing cliffs and is popular as a weekend venue for boats from Poole. It is also convenient for yachts that are heading east and awaiting the flood to carry them past St Alban's Head. Five miles further west, Kimmeridge Bay should be safe in a northerly wind but is cluttered by rock ledges. Beyond this, the sea has devoured the soft sands and clays, which lie between a coastal band of hard limestone and a parallel chalk ridge, to form a series of really spectacular anchorages.

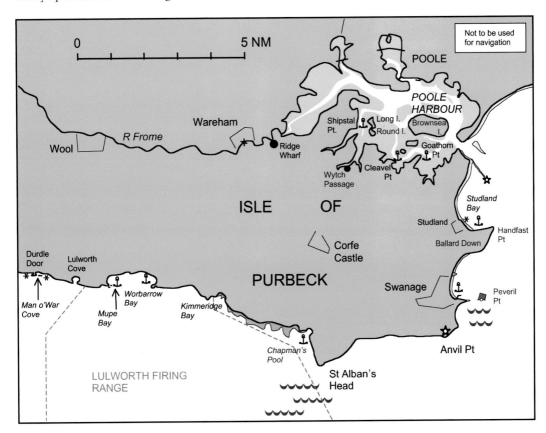

Fig 15 Purbeck.

Worbarrow Bay

THIS HANDSOME BAY is in the middle of the Lulworth Gunnery Range, so access is only possible in non-firing periods. Fortunately, those generally include most weekends and the main school summer holiday periods. The pebble beach at the eastern end is popular with holidaymakers, who stroll down from the car park in the deserted village of Tyneham, but most of them are gone by mid-evening. As a consequence of military occupation, the rest of the hinterland is largely wild. A few walkers come along the coastal path and an occasional fisherman brings a rod to the shore. The place feels a long way from civilisation – almost primeval – and the scenery is unforgettable, dominated by huge, crumbling cliffs that are slashed white by the most recent falls of chalk.

Choice of anchoring position will be dictated by the wind direction and any anticipated wind shifts. At the eastern end, the prominent headland of Worbarrow Tout hooks around an anchorage that is sheltered from between north and south-east, although a prolonged south-easterly wind would send in swell. For our most recent visit to this corner, we drifted in with a hesitant, westerly sea breeze, anchored off the beach, and rowed ashore for an evening barbecue. We were nominally on a lee shore but the sea was almost flat, the breeze was fading and, as the sun set, our fire's thin column of smoke wavered and then started to blow out over the water. The offshore gradient wind was reasserting itself and we lay in shelter for the rest of the night.

Mupe Bay. The Mupe Rocks form an excellent breakwater.

At the western end of the bay, there are cliffs to the north and west, and conditions are usually fairly comfortable in WSW winds because the jagged Mupe Rocks form an excellent wave break. On several occasions we have used this anchorage after rounding Portland Bill with a stiff westerly wind. Even with rampant white horses galloping past the reef, the water in Mupe Bay has remained comparatively flat.

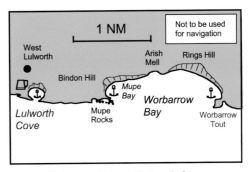

Fig 16 Worbarrow Bay and Lulworth Cove.

There are foreshore rocks off Worbarrow Tout and a submerged outlier close to the east of the Mupe Rocks, but the middle of the bay is free of obstacles. Along the northern shore, rock hazards come and go, as sections of the cliffs slide into the sea and are then slowly eroded. At each end the bottom is a mixture of sand, shingle, pebbles, boulders and some weed. The holding should be tested, to check that the anchor is holding on to something sensible, but we have never dragged in either anchorage. The tidal range is so small that it is usually possible to lie close inshore but on clear nights the high, sloping cliffs create sudden katabatic downdraughts, so that an anchored yacht will lunge around and jerk at her cable. Under these conditions, an anchorage in deep water will be more peaceful because there is some scope for the boat to move with each gust, resulting in less snatching.

On shore, within the range area, walkers must keep to the marked paths and not touch any metal objects. Landing is prohibited in the centre of the bay, at Arish Mell, but the coastal footpath is accessible from the beaches at either end, leading to breathtaking views from Bindon Hill or Rings Hill. On the latter, the ancient earthwork of Flowers Barrow was once a circular fortification but steady erosion has reduced it to a semicircle, its rampart and ditch neatly sectioned by the cliff edge. Half a mile west of Mupe Bay, a fossil forest of prehistoric tree stumps can be inspected, in a depression close to the edge of the cliffs. The low reef inshore of the Mupe Rocks is a rock pool paradise, although erosion of overlapping hollows in the limestone has given it some of the qualities of a scalloped knife, so inflatable dinghies should be handled carefully!

Lulworth Cove

THIS WELL-KNOWN BEAUTY SPOT is, in many ways, a less satisfactory anchorage than Worbarrow. Part of the problem is that the tide, as it flows past the mouth of the near-circular cove, causes the water within to rotate. Anchored boats tend to lie parallel with the beach and beam-on to the waves, which radiate inwards from the entrance. There are rocks on either side of the entrance and small boat moorings in the western half of the cove. On the eastern side, the holding seems to be good, in sand and clay, but this anchorage can become distinctly crowded in fine weather. In the event of an unexpected onshore wind, a departure through the narrow exit may be more difficult than from Worbarrow. However, Lulworth is outside the gunnery range. There is a pub, a freshwater tap by the car park, and provisions may be available in the village of West Lulworth.

Man o' War Cove. Not serious shelter but it makes an entertaining diversion.

Man o' War Cove

A COUPLE OF MILES WEST OF LULWORTH, the strata have been carved into another near-symmetrical inlet. This one is much smaller but is arguably even more picturesque. The outcrop of Durdle Door forms the western side of the cove. Man o' War Rock extends across the seaward side and is nearly joined to the cliffs, on the eastern side, by a sand bar that does not quite dry at low water.

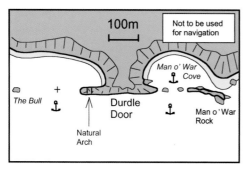

Fig 17 Man o' War Cove.

The cove is entered between Durdle Door and Man o' War Rock. Within the narrow gap, there is a drying rock on each side and the depth in the middle is *approximately* 1.4m. This figure should be regarded with caution as it was based on soundings taken with an oar and corrected by deducting the predicted height of tide. Broken tips of limestone were visible in the gap and prudent skippers should check soundings from their own dinghy before entering. Inside the cove, the greatest depth is about 2.3m, decreasing towards the beaches, but a drying ridge of rock extends from the shore in the south-west corner. There is room for about three yachts of modest size; this cannot be regarded as serious shelter but it makes for an entertaining diversion. On a fine day, swimmers should find that the water in the cove is warmer than in the rest of the English Channel.

Skippers with larger yachts or greater caution can anchor outside, where the outer face of the limestone forms an underwater cliff and the bottom drops away to level off at about 7m. To the west of Durdle Door, beyond its natural rock arch, the limestone ridge continues as a line of drying and submerged rocks. The only local 'facility' is an occasional ice cream van on the cliff top.

WEYMOUTH BAY

For yachts heading around Portland Bill, Lulworth or Worbarrow make good departure points in fine weather and offshore winds, when there is little to be gained by diverting to Weymouth. However, in south-west winds, there is better shelter in Weymouth Bay, north of the harbour. At the eastern corner of the Isle of Portland, the slight indentation of Church Ope Cove is sometimes used as a waiting anchorage, but it is often affected by swell and landing by dinghy may be hazardous. From anywhere in Weymouth Bay, it is fairly easy to time a passage so as to reach the Bill at slack water, because an eddy flows down the eastern side of Portland for the last few hours of the flood.

PORTLAND BILL TO TORBAY

Given fine weather and offshore winds, this northern portion of Lyme Bay is an attractive area for pottering between the small harbours, well away from most yachting traffic. One can anchor almost anywhere, clear of the foreshore rocks, but only if the land is to windward and the swell is slight. Few of the coastal anchorages gain much additional protection from local headlands. Beer Head provides enhanced shelter from the west but little from the south-west. Nevertheless, the bold chalk outcrop does seem to absorb some swell and Beer is a charming town to visit, provided that the sea is sufficiently calm for landing by dinghy on the steep pebble beach. Further west, the coves north of Hope's Nose enjoy some shelter from south-west but are overlooked by the suburbs of Torquay. There is, however, one other anchorage that deserves particular mention, if only because it is rarely visited.

Chesil Cove

CHESIL IS THE ONLY PLACE IN LYME BAY to offer good shelter from easterly winds and is a very convenient passage anchorage, where eastbound yachts can await a favourable tide for rounding Portland Bill. Most vessels would be unlikely to call here for any other reason, because this was a notorious lee-shore trap for sailing ships and its grim reputation is complemented by the scenery; both the unyielding uniformity of the pebble bank and the brutal rock faces of the Isle of Portland.

Hardly a picturesque cove, Chesil still provides a fascinating insight into the operation of beach-launched boats under the most unpromising circumstances. The traditional local fishing craft was the Portland lerret, clinker built and double ended. Its oars were elegant pieces of joinery, with pear-shaped balancing blocks and worked on single, iron thole pins. Single pins are also found on Northumberland cobles, Irish curraghs and Portuguese beach boats, all of which are intended to be launched and recovered in surf. The oars are more secure than in crutch rowlocks and a breaking sea can swing them fore-and-aft without risk of damage. Nowadays, the small boats at Chesil are either clinker with transom sterns or are constructed of GRP, but most are still equipped with the traditional pattern of oar.

The recovery of a boat returning to the shore requires considerable skill. Even when swell height is modest, waves break all along the beach but some parts of it are so steep that the incoming crests only heap up and collapse at the last moment. Typically, a boat is backed briefly into the pebbles so that one of the crew can leap ashore while the bow is still floating over deeper water, outside the surf line. He unreels a cable from a winch at the top of the beach, leaving surplus cable at the water's edge while he starts the winch motor. As the slack in the cable is taken up, the boat is again backed in and the cable is hooked on to a 'start rope', the other end of which is permanently fastened to the keel. Given good timing, the boat then slides smoothly up the beach, oars trailing, before the waves can turn and broach it.

Local fishermen can get ashore without even wetting their feet but landing and re-embarking in a yacht tender will be more hazardous unless the sea is practically flat. A small dinghy is quite likely to be dumped heavily on to the beach by a breaking wave. It may be possible to ram it on to the pebbles and jump out quickly, but most dinghies will be damaged by such treatment. Anyone who jumps into the water before the boat touches the beach, or who later attempts to hold the dinghy afloat while his companions re-board it, may well sink up to his neck if he treads on the loose edge of a submerged slope. However, the shoreline seamanship at Chesil is certainly relevant to the handling of yacht tenders on open beaches. This topic will be examined in more detail in Chapter 6.

TORBAY TO BOLT HEAD

South of Hope's Nose, the coastline becomes more deeply indented. It is generally sheltered from the north-west, and three of the anchorages described below also enjoy some protection from south-westerlies. For east winds, there are deepwater anchorages in the Dart and Salcombe estuaries, which are covered in Chapter 8.

Churston Cove

IN THE DAYS OF SAILING WARSHIPS, Torbay made an excellent anchorage for the Channel Fleet. Small yachts, on the other hand, find it wide and draughty. There are feasible anchorages against the western and northern shores but few of these are peaceful. Off the beaches, lines of buoys denote the bathing zones and late night excursion boats charge along just to seaward of the buoys. With music systems at full volume and disco lights flashing, their skippers could be forgiven for failing to spot a yacht's riding light against the shore illuminations. Elberry Cove in the south-west corner is clear of the tripper boat track but is a water-skiing area.

In winds between WSW and SE, we have found the best anchorage to be just west of Brixham Harbour. There is room for a few yachts inside the tiny Churston Cove but more space outside, where the shore is steep-to and the seabed drops away to a depth of about 5m. The Brixham fairway buoys lead coastal traffic clear of this area and the wooded shore produces a good patch of calm. Within the

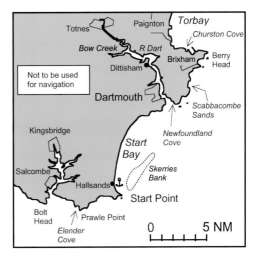

Fig 18 South-east Devon.

cove, the middle has a depth of 1.5m and a clay bottom, but the drying edges are partly covered by broken rocks, the residue of former quarrying activity, so care is needed when going ashore at low tide. The coastal footpath leads along the shore and provisioning parties may take a short stroll into Brixham, passing the hospitable Brixham YC along the way.

Churston Cove, with Brixham Harbour beyond.

Scabbacombe Sands

BETWEEN BERRY HEAD AND THE MOUTH OF THE DART, several large lumps of Devon rock lie up to a mile from the coast but there are also some pleasant beach anchorages. Scabbacombe Sands is particularly attractive because access to the beach from the land side entails a fairly long walk, so it is rarely overpopulated. Half a mile north of the anchorage, the Druids Mare (or Cod Rocks) dries by 2.9m. Half a mile to the south, Nimble Rock is covered by only 1.0m. A yacht that approaches the southern end of the beach on 270° should be well clear of both hazards. Between Berry Head and Scabbacombe, there are alternative anchorages off Man Sands and in St Mary's Bay, each having some rocks to seaward.

Newfoundland Cove

ON EITHER SIDE OF THE RIVER DART'S ENTRANCE, small coves offer shelter from northerly winds and provide possible venues for swimming or sandcastle building, although they are open to swell. The western coves become shaded by the cliffs during the afternoon but Newfoundland Cove, on the eastern side, faces the sun for most of each day.

Hallsands

THE NEXT MAJOR TIDAL GATE IS START POINT and the nearest waiting anchorage, for westerly winds, is immediately to the north, off the ruined village of Hallsands. While the Channel flood is flowing eastwards, an eddy develops in Start Bay and a boat that is approaching from the east can avoid the main tidal stream by standing well inshore, towards the middle of the bay. This should lead her into the counter current, flowing south to the Start.

The tapering crook of land wraps well around the southern end of the bay, creating an obvious and beautiful anchorage. Beautiful but bold: there is absolutely no hint of cosiness and the view to the east is all sky and horizon. The proximity of the Start Point tide race emphasises the exposed nature of this stretch of coast but, despite the untamed backdrop, the anchorage has many desirable features. The beach shelves steeply, so that yachts can lie quite close to the shore. There is unlimited room to anchor and predictable holding in sand and shingle. If the wind backs to south or south-east, Dartmouth is a convenient bolthole and retreat is downwind. The only drawback is swell, which finds its way around the Start and into the bay during strong south-west winds.

The remnants of Hallsands, fractured skeletons of houses clinging to rocks above the beach, may appear rather alarming to anyone who has misgivings about all that open sea to the east, yet its destruction owed more to human folly than to natural forces. The place was a successful fishing community until, in 1897, shingle was removed for use in the extension of Devonport Dockyard. By 1902 the beach level had dropped by 4m and by 1917 storms had substantially ruined the village, although a few buildings have survived at the northern end. Thankfully, the locals were eventually paid compensation. For

The ruined fishing village of Hallsands. The anchorage is close to the shore, tucked in behind Start Point.

modern sailors, one lesson to be drawn from those events is that, despite the lack of shelter to the east, the roadstead had enjoyed sufficient protection to enable the fishermen to operate from an open beach – until the Admiralty interfered.

When the tide is flowing west, the Start tidal race occurs where the stream crosses an underwater ridge to the east of the point. In rough weather it is advisable to keep at least a mile offshore and there may also be overfalls at the southern edge of the Skerries Bank, which lies in the middle of Start Bay. However, given reasonably good weather and sea conditions, there is a possible short cut towards the west, via the roadstead off Hallsands. In the open sea, south of Start Point, the tide turns to the west at about HW Dover −0130. Closer inshore, the favourable stream begins about an hour earlier, when the Start Bay eddy pushes past the point. On several occasions, in moderate westerly winds and swell, we have rounded the point near to the land before the main race has formed and with only a moderately lumpy sea where the eddy has been meeting the incoming waves. This is a typical example of a tidal gate with a waiting anchorage immediately downstream. With correct timing, one can make the most of the favourable stream and get ahead of the overfalls. Take care to keep clear of the Blackstone, which lies south of the point.

Elender Cove

THIS LITTLE CLEFT IN THE CLIFFS could hardly be classed as a haven but in fine weather it is a delightful spot for swimming and sunbathing. Pedestrian access from the top of the cliffs is difficult, so most of its customers come by boat from Salcombe, although landing is only possible if the swell is minimal. Situated immediately west of Prawle Point and sheltered from the north-east, the inlet also serves as a waiting anchorage for eastbound yachts when the tide is foul, the wind has faded or is on the nose, and there is a choice between burning fuel or … swimming and sunbathing.

6 Big Swell

Off south-west Devon, Cornwall and western Brittany, ocean swell is much more prominent than in the central English Channel. It often creates lumpy sea conditions for coastal sailing, causes a nuisance in some anchorages and may even be hazardous close to the shore. For pleasurable cruising in these waters, we need to know when and where to expect it and how to avoid it.

Swell waves are those that persist after the wind that generated them has ceased to blow, or that propagate into areas where the weather conditions are different. In the Channel, east winds have only a limited fetch, from the Straits of Dover, and their leftover waves usually pass through and clear the area within about 24 hours. Ocean swell, on the other hand, is created by depressions in the Atlantic and can be detected on most days of the year, the waves generally coming in from the wide-open westerly quadrant between Ouessant and Ireland.

As described in Chapter 4, wave motion in the open sea consists of a spectrum of short, medium and long wavelengths. If such waves propagate away from an Atlantic depression, those with the longer wavelengths travel faster and the short waves are left behind, where they become mixed up with new waves created by the next weather system. Sometimes the long waves arrive on the coasts of Europe well before the depression that created them, or the depression tracks away to the north so that the swell appears to be completely divorced from the observed weather.

Swell refraction

Swell waves entering the western Channel often have a period (the time between successive crests) of 10 seconds or more. The relationship between period and wavelength is:

Wavelength (in metres) = 1.56 x period (in seconds) squared

Therefore, in deep water, 10-second waves have a wavelength of 156 metres. If we accept the rule of thumb that they will 'feel the bottom' in a depth equal to approximately half their wavelength (ie 78 metres), we can expect such waves to become noticeably slowed and distorted while they are still a long way offshore.

When swell waves roll over an undersea bank, as shown in Figure 19, they are refracted in the usual way, so that their crests swing in towards the shallower water. This concentrates the wave energy over the bank, where the swell becomes steeper, with a greater likelihood of breaking crests. Conversely if swell passes between two shallow areas, the wave energy is refracted outwards and the deeper water becomes calmer. If a yacht is heading inshore in heavy swell, it may therefore be possible to avoid the steepest seas by steering clear of 'convex' depth contours and favouring the deeper gullies.

After swell has passed over a bank, the wave pattern usually becomes disjointed, with irregular, crossing seas that make for uncomfortable sailing.

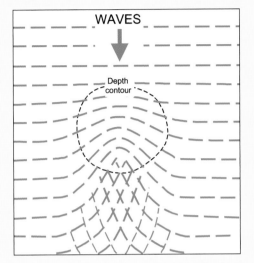

However, a group of such banks will break up and disperse the swell, providing useful protection to any anchorages that lie further inshore.

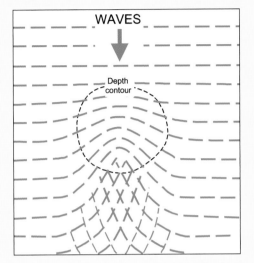

Fig 19 Swell refraction over a submerged bank.

Very long swell

The term 'ground swell' is commonly used to describe swell that seems to rear out of a calm sea, arriving without warning to create mayhem on bathing beaches or even to damage sea defences. There is nothing mysterious about this phenomenon, which is associated with swell of a very long wavelength, usually the product of a distant storm. In deep water the long, low swell is scarcely noticeable but if it enters the shallows without being disrupted by offshore banks, the wave train is foreshortened, the height of the waves increases and there is enough energy to produce large crests. Therefore, breakers caused by very long swell often occur above relatively smooth, shelving seabeds.

Where there is a shallow sand bar at the mouth of an estuary, an ebb tide flowing out of the river will generally create the worst sea conditions but swell alone may be a hazard, even at high water. If a yacht is in shoaling water and regular, widely spaced crests become more noticeable among the shorter waves, that is a warning that swell is starting to build.

Drying harbours

Around the West Country and on the coast of Brittany, there are many small, drying harbours with walls that do not extend into deep water. On a yacht equipped with twin keels or legs, it is tempting to regard such places as potential refuges but they may be unsafe in swell.

In a typical small harbour on an exposed coastline, the resident boats are of shallow draught and are moored fore-and-aft, clear of the masonry, so that they merely surge to and fro if swell enters the harbour and pushes them around. As the tide falls, the swell starts to break outside the harbour and the water within becomes calmer, allowing them to take the ground gently. A yacht, unless she is of very shallow draught, may touch the bottom while the water is still deep enough to admit the swell, causing her to pound before coming to rest.

Low-tide protection

When choosing an anchorage, we usually look for a barrier of land to windward. If the anchorage dries and is in an area subject to swell, it is also advisable to select a spot where the yacht will not take the ground until offshore rocks have uncovered.

Some coastal communities, mostly in Brittany, enjoy such good natural protection from their surrounding rocks that they have managed to do without artificial harbour walls. At low tide the reefs are uncovered and the mooring areas are calm. Most of the rocks cover at high tide and the moorings are then exposed to the open sea but the submerged reefs disrupt large waves. As long as the local boats cannot bump against anything solid, they are allowed to dance around on their tethers. However, their owners do not sleep on board; for cruisers, this kind of shelter will be uncomfortable unless sea conditions are placid.

Going ashore by dinghy

A low swell may be tolerable in a deep-water anchorage but is likely to break on the beach, hindering any attempt to go ashore by dinghy. If there is a harbour wall, its steps or a ladder should enable the crew to land dry-shod unless there is a heavy surge. On an open beach, landing and re-embarking in a tender requires some forethought unless the sea is practically flat.

The aim is to spend as little time as possible in the surf zone; in this context, 'surf' refers to any breaking waves. Under fairly calm conditions, the wavelets may have crests that only reach bathers' knees, but it is still possible for a dinghy to be dumped heavily on the sand and swamped if it is not handled skilfully. Reaching dry land is one thing but re-launching is often more difficult, with the dinghy having to be lifted to floating depth and then held steady for everyone to board. If the sea is breaking more heavily than expected, re-embarkation may be impossible, which will be inconvenient with the yacht lying at anchor.

Before heading in to the beach, it is advisable to hold the dinghy in deep water and assess wave conditions, remembering that breaking crests look less impressive when viewed from behind. Are there any foreshore rocks to act as breakwaters? In some coves there may be a calm corner, or even a square rock to serve as a landing jetty. Oars normally give better control than an outboard motor and passengers should be briefed to step out quickly in the shallows and pick up the dinghy.

Temporary calm

Many coastal anchorages become calmer as the tide falls and some are popular as low water picnic spots. There may be two reasons for the calm conditions. First, where rocks and offshore reefs become uncovered, they act as solid breakwaters.

Second, if the tide is flowing against the waves or swell, the current acts as a liquid breakwater by refracting the waves away from the shore (see Chapter 4). In some places – notably northern Brittany and parts of the Channel Islands – the two effects coincide because there are plenty of rocks and the tide flows to the west, against the Atlantic swell, during most of the period when the level is falling. When the tide turns, rocks will continue to provide protection until they cover but the effect of refraction reverses more quickly. In places with no off-lying reefs conditions can deteriorate suddenly, so that an anchored yacht develops a violent roll and members of the crew who have gone ashore have to re-launch the dinghy in breaking waves.

These effects vary from day to day, depending on the strength of the current and the size and direction of the swell. Do not be deterred from visiting these beautiful anchorages but always be alert to a change in sea state, particularly at the turn of the tide.

Rolling stones

Big waves can move loose boulders. Where this represents a rearrangement of a rubble-covered foreshore, it is of little significance to navigation. However, there are some places where isolated rocks have been shifted or rolled, so that a few of the 'drying rock' symbols on the charts are out of date. I am aware of instances in Cornwall, the Isles of Scilly and Brittany, which will be mentioned in the appropriate chapters, but there are likely to be others. All the examples observed were rocks on sandbanks that were exposed to swell from the west.

Bolt Head to Land's End

We are now moving from the soft south of Britain to the slightly wilder west. The weather tends to be a little damper and the waves are lumpier but the old fishing villages and rock-girt coves offer the prospect of dozens of delightful anchorages. Most of the pilotage is straightforward and there are more opportunities for eyeball navigation because the seawater becomes clearer as we approach the Atlantic. In some of the anchorages, the best holding is on areas of sand, between patches of rock, and it is often possible to distinguish between the two.

Very few of the coastal bays provide shelter from the south but most cover either west-and-north or east-and-north, with the former predominating because the general trend of the coast is towards WSW. If the wind insists on blowing from the south, or the sea is too rough for lying in open bays, the long, navigable estuaries are available for us to explore, and we'll do just that in Chapter 8.

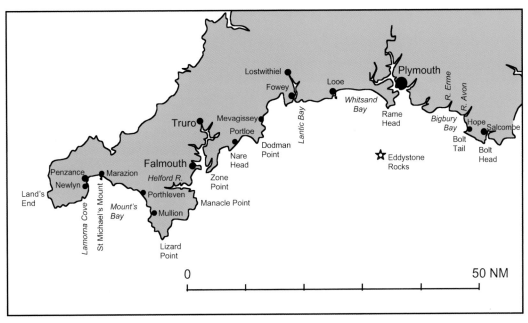

Fig 20 Bolt Head to Land's End.

BIGBURY BAY

When a yacht is beating into a westerly wind and depression drizzle, this deep indentation is an uninviting lee shore with difficult river entrances, to be left safely astern as soon as possible. On other days, with sunshine and an offshore wind, the bay shrugs off its air of grey menace and becomes friendly and accommodating. From the passing yacht, observers notice that the cliffs are modest affairs, interspersed with green slopes and stretches of sand. Why hurry past?

Hope Cove

THIS IS THE FIRST COASTAL ANCHORAGE WEST OF CHESIL COVE to provide really good shelter from easterly winds. In the days of commercial sail as many as 60 vessels might be found lurking in the lee of Bolt Tail, waiting for a favourable shift to help them up Channel. As at Chesil, a sudden veer could be deadly and it was essential to head for open

Hope Cove at low water. Half Tide Rock is in the middle of the photograph and the yacht indicates the usual anchorage position.

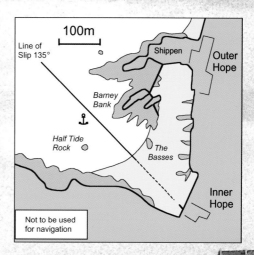

water if there was any risk of becoming embayed. In settled conditions beach-launched boats could be moored on a patch of sand protected by the Barney Bank, a cluster of large rocks on the seaward side of the beach, and there are records of a settlement here in the thirteenth century. A concrete breakwater now links the Barney Bank to the shore but it cannot exclude big waves and local craft are hauled on to the quayside when bad weather threatens.

Yachts usually anchor outside the harbour, roughly west of the breakwater end. The principal hazards are Half Tide Rock, which lies about 100m off the southern shore, and the rock tails that extend from the Barney Bank.

Fig 21 Hope Cove.

The old lifeboat house, in the south-east corner of the cove, has a slip that is aligned on about 135° and this appears to indicate a safe approach line. At neaps there should be sufficient water for a shoal-draught yacht to lie afloat nearer to the harbour, but care must be taken to avoid the Basses and other low outcrops close to the harbour entrance. There is no chart on a scale greater than 1:75,000 and therefore, for reassurance, use of this inner anchorage requires an actual sighting of Half Tide Rock, in order to check that there is sufficient swinging room.

In the eighteenth century, the income of the local fishing community was heavily supplemented by smuggling. To curb the illicit trade, coastguard cottages were built at the head of the harbour and there was a lookout post on top of the Shippen promontory… until it fell over the edge, during one particularly dark and stormy night. Did it fall or was it pushed? In 1823 a group of fishermen's wives were imprisoned for assaulting a coast-guard officer who had interrupted their tax evasion. They evidently regarded this as a challenge and, upon their release, it seems that the gaol's copper cooking pots accompanied them to freedom. Nowadays the village has become respectable and the main occupations include golf, retirement and holidays of the quieter type. The harbour side is a cheerful place, with two pubs, a Post Office store and a freshwater tap on the quay.

Erme Mouth

THE BED OF THE SAND-FILLED ERME ESTUARY is privately owned and visiting boats have been discouraged from entering the inner reaches but there is a deepwater anchorage at the mouth, inshore of the Mary's Rocks and sheltered from winds between north-west and east.

The West and East Mary's Rocks dry by 1.1m and 1.5m respectively and a clear channel, about 200m wide, lies between the former rock and Battisborough Island, which looks as if it is joined to the western cliffs. When West Mary's Rock is covered, it is possible to enter the estuary by approaching from the south-west and passing fairly close to Battisborough Island. At low springs, when West Mary's Rock is uncovered, one can simply steer between it and Battisborough Island. However, Edwards' Rock (1.1m) lies further offshore and will then be close to the surface. There is a feasible entrance transit: a ruined limekiln, on the east bank and close to the narrowest part of the estuary, open of Owen's Hill on about 048°. Unfortunately, the limekiln is becoming overgrown and is difficult to identify until one has reached the anchorage, by which time its usefulness is diminished!

The usual anchorage position is SSW of Owen's Hill, off a small beach below the

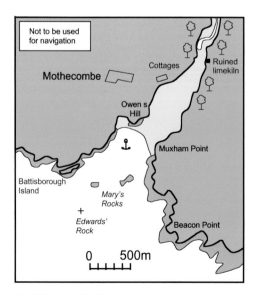

Fig 22 Erme Mouth.

hamlet of Mothecombe. The bottom is clean sand but depths should be checked carefully, as the river's low tide outflow channel moves around from time to time and the sand levels may change.

From the beach, a road leads inland through Mothecombe but this is only open to the public on certain days. A small public lane reaches the river north of Owen's Hill, close to some former coastguard cottages. In the early nineteenth century, a gravel spit extended from this part of the western shore, almost closing the river entrance, and was used for holding local fairs. Now the mouth of the estuary is completely open and wild – no facilities or fairs whatsoever.

PLYMOUTH SOUND

For a yacht making an overnight stop during a coastal cruise, the city of Plymouth is an unprofitable diversion. Of the three marinas, the one in Sutton Harbour is inside a lock gate and the others are some distance away from the main attractions. If the wind is in the west, many experienced voyagers prefer to anchor on the Cornish side of the Sound.

Cawsand Bay

THIS IS A VERY UNCOMPLICATED ANCHORAGE: shelter from the west, fairly predictable holding, few significant hazards and a pair of relatively unspoilt villages with a selection of pubs. The twin settlements of Cawsand and Kingsand have resisted the influence of the tourist industry better than some other parts of Cornwall because road access from Plymouth entails a long detour around the tributaries of the Tamar estuary. In addition to pubs, the villages have several shops and there is usually a public freshwater tap, although its location seems to vary.

The bay has ample room for anchoring except at weekends, when Cawsand is a Saturday night destination for local yachts. It is overlooked by high ground and strong winds generate sharp gusts so allow a generous scope of anchor cable. If the wind backs towards south, swell comes in around Penlee Point. The calmest conditions are then found close to the wooded southern shore, but take care not to foul the local moorings and floating keep boxes which are concentrated in that area.

Sir Francis Drake might have difficulty in recognising the modern city of Plymouth but he would feel at home off Cawsand, where nothing has changed that would affect the operation of sailing vessels. There are more houses crammed

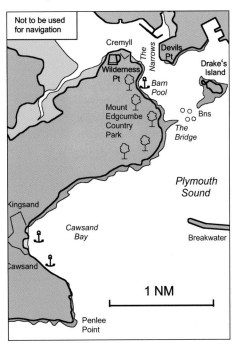

Fig 23 Cawsand Bay and Barn Pool.

into the head of the bay, and a couple of modern Victorian forts, but anyone swinging at anchor will be mindful of the same winds and tides that governed the actions of Tudor seamen. Drake was by no means the only swashbuckler of his time and many of the powerful families who dominated Cornish politics in the fifteenth and sixteenth centuries were dabbling in privateering or piracy. Some of them managed the transition to more peaceful commercial activity and their estates still exist, although a few are now in public occupation. One of the best examples is found at our next anchorage.

Barn Pool

THE RIVER TAMAR DISCHARGES INTO PLYMOUTH SOUND through The Narrows between the rocky bluff of Devil's Point and Wilderness Point, with its rather decorative Garden Battery that once guarded the approaches to the naval dockyard. The main channel snakes around the eastern side of Drake's Island, which is linked to the Cornish shore by a line of shoals and military obstacles known as The Bridge. This is crossed by a small boat channel marked by beacons, which has a depth of about 2m.

Between The Bridge and Wilderness Point, the old Mount Edgcumbe estate overlooks Barn Pool, wrapping around the anchorage as if it were a marine amphitheatre. This place positively oozes history. In Tudor times, long before the Garden Battery was conceived, Mount Edgcumbe was regarded as having 'the noblest prospect in all England' and the

Barn Pool, in Plymouth Sound, is cradled in the natural amphitheatre of the Mount Edgcumbe Country Park.

Duke of Medina Sidonia, commander-in-chief of the Spanish Armada, who knew of its reputation, planned to make it his English home. If that had come to pass, the Edgcumbe family would not have been entirely innocent victims, for a few years earlier, while England and Spain were at peace, some Spanish ships had run aground on the Bridge. Peter Edgcumbe was away from home so his wife mustered the servants and led them down to the shore – not on a rescue mission but to loot the cargoes.

Much later, Mount Edgcumbe House did suffer from enemy action when it was burnt by Luftwaffe incendiaries. However, the estate exacted revenge by helping to launch an invasion in the opposite direction. It served as an embarkation point for D-Day and the beach at Barn Pool was covered by landing craft loading ramps. The old house has since been restored and the last of the rectangular, concrete ramp segments are now stacked along the sea wall.

Barn Pool can be a somewhat tricky anchorage. There is shelter from between south-west and north, plus fair protection from the Plymouth shore to the north-east. It lies just clear of the strong flood and ebb streams but eddies swirl into the anchorage and cause yachts to range around – behaviour that may be exacerbated when strong westerly winds cause random gusts to drop on to the water from the high ground.

Much of the seabed slopes steeply towards very deep water, where there are soundings in excess of 30m, and consists partly of rock and loose shale, giving very poor holding. Nevertheless, there is an area with good holding in the northern part of the bay, on a fairly level ledge of muddy sand or gravel at a depth of about 6m. An obstruction lies at the outer limit of this ledge and is shown on large-scale charts. An anchor tripping line is usually recommended because of wartime debris on the bottom. We usually dispense with this precaution because the vagaries of wind and tide can cause a yacht to over-ride and become tangled with its anchor buoy. However, yachts have anchored here success-fully with tripping lines lightly seized to their anchor cables.

If you can anchor securely, the magnificent surroundings should be adequate com-pensation for the effort. The estate is now the Mount Edgcumbe Country Park, leased to Plymouth City and Cornwall County Councils, so waterborne visitors may land on the beach and explore. Turn south and climb to the shoulder of the hill, on which a skeletal folly is a thoughtfully located vantage point with views across to Plymouth Hoe and up the Tamar Valley. Closer to the anchorage, the estate's splendid orangery now serves as a tearoom and restaurant. If that is closed, turn north through the gardens to the hamlet of Cremyll, where the Edgcumbe Arms stands a few yards from Mashfords' famous boatyard.

ANCHORAGES BETWEEN FOWEY AND DODMAN POINT

For fifteen miles to the west of Plymouth Sound, the coastal bays provide little shelter from winds other than north. Looe Bay is tenable in a gentle westerly and the eastern corner of Lantic Bay is adequate in stiff easterlies but beyond Fowey there is a much better selection of anchorages.

Polridmouth

POLRIDMOUTH COVE IS OVERLOOKED by Daphne du Maurier's one-time home of Menabilly and may have provided part of the setting for her novel *Rebecca*, with Menabilly House being 'Manderley'. It is mainly used as a picnic anchorage on days when there is a flat sea and an offshore wind, but is included here because it provides an illustration of the 'rolling stones' phenomenon that was mentioned in Chapter 6.

Close to the east of Gribbin Head, there are sandbanks that change their positions and shapes. This can be confirmed by a study of old charts, different editions of which indicate shallow areas in different places. At one time, a drying rock was shown in the mouth of Polridmouth Cove; at the time of our last visit, there was a 2m deep pool in that position. This suggests that the drying rock was not connected to bedrock but was a weed-covered boulder, resting on a transient bank of sand. Boats usually anchor outside the cove; it may be possible to lie afloat much closer to the beach but that depends on whether the sandbank has returned!

Polkerris

THIS IS AN EXCELLENT ANCHORAGE FOR EAST WINDS, when remarkably effective shelter can be found close to the shore, just south of the drying harbour. Directly outside the harbour, the sand is only about 0.5m below chart datum. Between Polkerris and Little Gribbin the coastline appears to be fairly clean, with no detached hazards shown on the charts. The beach in the shallow bay between Little Gribbin and Gribbin Head looks attractive but there are several very nasty rocks and possibly some more loose boulders.

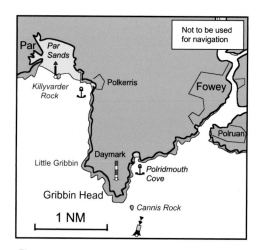

Fig 24 Polridmouth and Polkerris.

In the event of a wind shift towards south, the nearest bolthole is Fowey. Par Harbour is strictly commercial while at Charlestown, two miles to the west, the only secure shelter is in the gated basin and entry via the small outer basin would be unsafe in strong onshore winds. Both these harbours have drying approaches.

Polkerris has a small store and a pub, the Rashleigh Inn, named after the local family, who were Tudor contemporaries of the Edgcumbes and who remain the local landlords. There was once a very prosperous fishing fleet and large, ruined pilchard cellars are set behind the harbour. The fish and the fishing faded away in the mid nineteenth century, the Polkerris lifeboat was later moved to Fowey, and the little hamlet has been snoozing ever since.

Portmellon

ON THE WESTERN SIDE OF ST AUSTELL BAY there are several secondary bays, tucked in behind Dodman Point, which provide effective shelter from westerly winds. The series of projecting headlands appears to absorb energy from incoming swell, as these bays often seem to be comparatively placid. At Portmellon, the usual anchorage is off the middle of the small, sandy cove but if the wind is from south-west there is likely to be some swell, in which case a position closer to Chapel Point may be more comfortable. If a light to moderate wind backs to due south, the point continues to provide some shelter but a flopper stopper is definitely required.

On shore, there is a pub and also a boat-yard, from which newly built yachts have been launched into the cove. As Portmellon is only half a mile south of Mevagissey, it is close enough for quick access to the shops – but is likely to be much more peaceful. Admittedly, it offers no shelter in east winds, but some would say that for visiting yachts, Mevagissey Harbour is not much better in that respect.

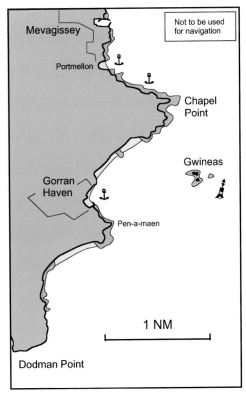

Fig 25 Portmellon and Gorran Haven.

Gorran Haven

THE ENTRANCE TO THIS BAY is partly obstructed by the Gwineas Rocks but their three main heads are exposed to view at MHWS and an east cardinal buoy marks their offshore side. There is a recognised tidal race off Dodman Point, although it is rarely apparent in fine weather, probably because the tidal streams are relatively weak. The shoals off the point have depths of about 6m and we have often sailed over them with the current creating hardly a ripple. However, bad weather and large waves stir the cauldron much more vigorously.

Gorran is not quite so well protected as Portmellon but the anchorage is usually very pleasant in winds from west or north-west. The bottom is clean, gently shelving sand and there is a small stone pier, which can be useful for going ashore when low swell is breaking on the beach. Local boats occupy most of the drying harbour, although there may be room for a visiting yacht to go temporarily alongside the wall, close to the steps. Good fenders are essential for protection against the rough masonry. On shore, there is a freshwater tap in the boat compound and a shop and pubs in the village.

Gorran Haven's harbour was originally developed by the Bodrugan family, whose name is commemorated in the farmstead of Bodrugan Barton, above Chapel Point. The

Gorran Haven. There is plenty of swinging room to seaward of the drying harbour.

Bodrugans were rivals of the Edgcumbes and they supported opposite sides in the Wars of the Roses. After the Battle of Bosworth in 1485, Richard Edgcumbe (ancestor of Peter) was knighted by the victorious Henry VII and promptly came to arrest Sir Henry Bodrugan, who had clearly backed the wrong horse, or the wrong king. The term 'arrest' may conjure up a gentlemanly image of a firm hand on the collar, but in the fifteenth century it was likely to be a more robust business and Sir Henry didn't wait to find out, but fled over the cliff, boarded a waiting boat and sailed into exile. His place of departure, just south of Chapel Point, is still known as 'Bodrugan's Leap'.

ROSELAND PENINSULA

The Roseland Peninsula, a place of quiet beauty, lies between the sea and the River Fal. On the western side of Carrick Roads, at Falmouth and around Mylor and Restronguet Creeks, most of the sheltered deep water is crowded by moorings and overlooked by housing. The Roseland shore is much more sleepy, however, and there are also a couple of coastal village anchorages that are normally by-passed by yachts on passage.

Portloe

BETWEEN DODMAN POINT AND NARE HEAD, Veryan Bay has some attractive beaches but its western shore is a forbidding line of gaunt cliffs. From the south-east, a few houses can be glimpsed through a cleft: this is the dramatic entrance to Portloe, which epitomises the Cornish fishing village in miniature. If it did not exist, anyone who painted its image would be regarded as an utterly fanciful romantic.

Given a calm sea and an offshore wind, the initial approach is straightforward. Lath Rock, a mile to the south-east, is covered by 2m; it may cause heavy swell to break but nobody in his right mind would approach Portloe in heavy swell. The entrance is tiny and even a slight swell here is noticeable as a surge, heaving over the foreshore rocks. A yacht lying within the cleft on one anchor might swing against the rocks, and anchors fore and aft could obstruct access for local boats, so it is better to anchor outside and go in by dinghy.

The narrow inlet doglegs to port, out of sight, and terminates in a sandy beach. A short breakwater juts from the cliff but boats are normally drawn clear of the water and on to a concrete apron. These small craft work for their living and the harbour, although picturesque, is possessed of a purposeful atmosphere. The beach-facing wall of the Lugger Hotel has been well washed by the sea, although its landward side offers a hospitable welcome. Alternative refreshments are available from the Tregain Tea Room, on the other side of the slip.

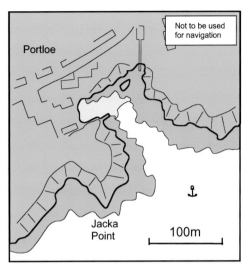

Fig 26 Portloe.

Portloe is so compact that it is advisable to anchor outside the cleft and go ashore by dinghy.

Portloe was a harbour that tried to operate a lifeboat, but failed. The first boathouse was beside the beach and the second above a steep slip, still visible in the northern corner of the inlet. For 17 years the station performed no successful service because in rough weather conditions in the harbour entrance were invariably too severe to permit launching.

Portscatho

PORTLOE'S OUTSIDE ANCHORAGE has no barrier against swell from the west and will often be too agitated for a prolonged stay. Five miles to the south-west, Portscatho offers somewhat better protection, with a slightly indented bay in a coast that is aligned north-to-south. Its frontage is rather plain but the foreshore is a good family playground, with both sand and rock pools. The drying rocks extend to seaward of the short breakwater, which is a relatively modern addition. The original beach was protected by its rocks until 1891, when the ship *Carl Hirschberg* drove ashore, almost ending up in the living room of one of the cottages. The ship was eventually released by blasting the rocks, but it was then necessary to construct the breakwater to supplement the depleted reef. There is a straight cleft through the outer rocks, which may have been the route of the *Carl Hirschberg*'s escape and which now serves as a small boat channel into the harbour at half-tide. The rock heads dry by about 3m on either side of this cleft and Portscatho is another place where yachts are best anchored offshore, leaving the harbour clear for small craft. The village has a selection of shops and pubs.

South of Portscatho, the Towan and Porthbeor beaches are suitable for anchoring and swimming in fine weather. Porthbeor has no car park and is unlikely to be crowded but there are scattered foreshore rocks, close to the low water line, which are not shown on the UKHO charts.

St Mawes

THE ROSELAND'S MAIN CENTRE OF POPULATION sits lightly in the landscape, possibly because its roadstead faces south-west and most of the local moorings are confined to the inner reaches of the Percuil River. This side of the Carrick Roads is most likely to be visited when the wind is easterly and then St Mawes is a convenient source of supplies, including excellent Cornish pasties. Freshwater is available from the St Mawes Sailing Club.

The anchorage is a real treat for yachtsmen who are more accustomed to cramped conditions. It has a fairly clean bottom, modest currents and plenty of swinging room, although fairways should be left clear for the St Mawes to Falmouth ferry and the sailing club start line, outside the small harbour.

St Just

ST JUST CREEK IS RENOWNED for its churchyard, an exotic jungle where alien plants flourish in the shelter of the steep hillside. It is a place of pilgrimage, both for the devout and for keen gardeners.

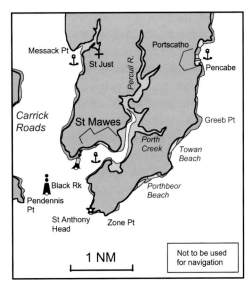

Most of the Carrick Roads is shallow but the Fal's winding gully of deeper water was nearly the ruination of St Just, where the channel bends close to the shore. This had long been used as a quarantine and laying-up anchorage, which prompted various schemes for harbour facilities. An eighteenth century plan for a naval dockyard was abandoned in favour of Devonport; a nineteenth century idea envisaged a railway terminus; and a twentieth century proposal was intended to serve transatlantic liners. Thankfully, every scheme lapsed and St Just retained its tranquillity.

The mouth of the creek is densely packed with moorings. Further in, mud alternates with firm banks of gravel and shoal-draught yachts could take the ground. Outside, there is room to anchor inshore of the deep channel, in a depth of about 2m and close to the beach. The bed has patches of loose stones or shells and we have experienced some difficulty in persuading a 'plough' anchor to set. However, when the point of an anchor has been properly dug in, the holding appears to be good.

Fig 27 The Roseland Peninsula.

EAST OF THE LIZARD

The eastern side of the Lizard Peninsula provides particularly good shelter from the prevailing winds. The Helford River is the main attraction, but in the Pool, off Helford village, the visitors' moorings are often fully occupied and anchoring space is restricted by the upstream oyster beds. Fortunately, there are several other quiet corners between Helford and the Lizard, which is the last major tidal gate on the south coast. Some of these bays and inlets are well protected from Atlantic weather while others, although more exposed, are convenient for short stops when one is bound westward and awaiting a favourable tide.

Helford River Entrance

WITHIN THE HELFORD RIVER but downstream of the Pool, it is possible to tuck into Ponsence Cove, close under the steep, wooded, southern shore. See Figure 28. We have lain at anchor here in complete calm while a strong southerly wind whistled overhead, tossing the trees but causing hardly a ripple on the water. Interestingly, during the ebb, the current flowed past to the north of the anchorage, leaving us in slack water, and the incoming swell, swinging into the river from the south, ran up the tongue of current. Boats heading out to sea were burying their bows in the swell while the cove remained placid, because refraction trapped the waves in the ebb stream.

For northerly winds, there is an equally good anchorage just west of Durgan, clear of a voluntary 'no anchoring' area that protects the eelgrass beds further east. From Ponsence

Cove or Durgan, it is only a short row into Helford, which has a Post Office store, a pub and the hospitable Helford River Sailing Club.

A mile to the south-east there is usually some space to anchor in the mouth of Gillan Creek. During our recent visits the local moorings have been located on the northern side of this inlet, leaving just enough room on the southern side for a yacht to anchor and swing. The sand levels vary, however, and we found one spot (which may have been rocky) where there was poor holding.

Just west of Ponsence Cove, the Voose rock extends from the southern shore and is normally marked by a north cardinal buoy. Right in the middle of the entrance to Gillan Creek, the Car Croc rock is normally marked by an east cardinal buoy. In each case the key word is 'normally', as either buoy may be absent from time to time.

Outside Gillan Creek, the quietly attractive Parbean Cove nestles behind Nare Point and is one of the very few south Cornish anchorages to enjoy some shelter from south-east. Although it is outside an estuary and largely free of silt, it is also shielded from westerly swell and luxuriant, multi-coloured seaweeds hang in the clear water. Rocks hook around the cove on both sides but there is a sandy patch in the middle.

The Helford area is now a summer retreat for the well-to-do but it once had a reputation for nefarious deeds. In her book *Frenchman's Creek*, Daphne du Maurier endowed the local buccaneers with a romantic image, but the people who practised the trade of piracy around the Helford were in fact at the scruffier end of the professional spectrum. The upper class pirates came from Falmouth where, in the sixteenth century, Sir John Killigrew was the principal landowner and also governor of Pendennis Castle. Simultaneously, his sons were operating as privateers and attacking Spanish ships, under the authority of French letters of marque (France was then at war with Spain but England was not). From privateering, it was a small step to full-blown piracy. Most conveniently, Sir John was appointed chairman of the government commission for investigating piracy, which greatly facilitated the family business. After one blatant attack on a Spanish vessel, the Privy Council decided to press its own investigations and discovered that the organiser of the outrage was Lady Killigrew. It seems that, among the Cornish gentry, the female of the species was at least as deadly as the male.

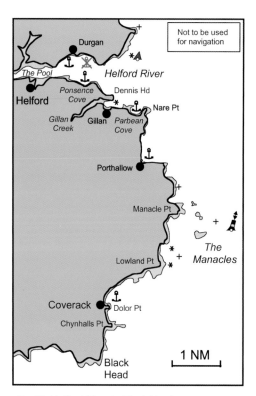

Fig 28 Helford River to Black Head.

Porthallow has no artificial harbour. The beach is sheltered from west and south.

Porthallow

THIS VILLAGE IS AT THE HEAD OF A DEEP, RIGHT-ANGLED RECESS in the coast and offers a good chance of a peaceful night. If swell is persisting after a westerly blow, the next (relatively) quiet anchorage is likely to be in the Isles of Scilly. There are no hazards within the bay, although a close approach to the narrow beach lies between drying rocks that extend from both the western and southern shores.

A few years ago, the village purchased the freehold of its foreshore from the local landowner and has since imported shingle to build up the beach, where boats are normally pulled well clear of the sea. Porthallow can supply many of the needs of a cruising yacht and there is even a marine engineer, just up the street past the pub and the Post Office store. The pub, the Five Pilchards, is well known for its display of photographs of wrecked ships, a reminder that the Manacles are just around the corner.

The Manacles

THIS IS A MINOR CLUSTER OF ROCKS in comparison to the reefs of Brittany, and yet it gained a fearsome record as a ship trap, largely because it lay close to the tracks of ships that were bound down-Channel or into Falmouth. The whole group covers at high water, with the marginal exception of the tip of Carn du (0.3m), and is marked by a single, east cardinal buoy, which may be difficult to spot in poor visibility. Tidal streams run through the reef at up to 2 knots, so it should be given a wide berth in bad weather.

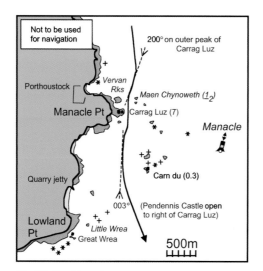

Fig 29 The Manacles.

In fine weather and slight swell, there is a possible inshore passage between the Manacles and the shore. A large-scale chart is essential, either No. 154, on a scale of 1:35,000, or No. 147. Between the reef and the prominent foreshore rock of Carrag Luz the northern end of the clear channel is almost 200m wide but there is a shortage of leading marks. Our own procedure, when coming from the north, is to approach the outer peak of Carrag Luz on a bearing of 200°, passing between the Vervan Rocks and Maen Chynoweth, both of which cover. There are no marks at all for clearing Carrag Luz, but the safe water is wider at this point and we steer to pass about 100m off, holding a course of 180° until south of the bulge of Manacle Point. The last part of the inshore passage has the best marks; the turret of Pendennis Castle (overlooking Falmouth) open of Carrag Luz on 003° clears the rocks off Lowland Point. On this leg, Carn du serves as a fairly prominent natural beacon, close to the south-west corner of the Manacles.

The most worrying hazard is Maen Chynoweth, which was recently struck by a lifeboat while on exercise. That rock only dries by 1.2m, however; if a yacht uses the inshore passage with the first of the south-going tide, the time will be close to local high water and the rock should be well covered. Between the Manacles and Lowland Point, quarried stone is loaded into coasters at a small jetty, and the coasters sometimes use this short cut.

Coverack

IF SWELL FROM THE ATLANTIC IS MODEST, then winds from between west and north produce reasonably sheltered conditions between the Manacles and the Lizard. The best-known anchorage is Coverack, which has another small, drying harbour with a single pier. The inner half of the bay is shallow, with some foreshore rocks close to chart datum, so it is advisable to anchor about 200m N or NNW of Dolor Point. Provisions can be purchased in the village.

Church Cove

A MILE OR SO EAST OF THE LIZARD, north of Hot Point, there is an excellent waiting anchorage in westerly winds. (See Figure 30.) Church Cove itself is little more than a crack in the cliffs with a very steep, rough concrete slipway, the toe of which drops away abruptly on to sand. The concrete cladding of a sewer outfall pipe forms a rough 'jetty' at some heights of tide and we have used this to disembark from a dinghy. However, there

Church Cove. The rough concrete of the outfall casing may serve as a jetty, although heavy swell would preclude landing.

may be a powerful surge from swell, perhaps sufficient to prevent landing altogether. Cadgwith, a mile to the north, could be an alternative place to go ashore but that would entail landing on a beach, which might not be any easier in swell.

Outside Church Cove, there is a group of small boat moorings but also room to anchor north or south of the outfall, the end of which is marked by a buoy. To the north, there appears to be more sand and less weed. A shallow rock lies close to the line of the outfall and the Craggan Rocks (covered by 1.5m) are half a mile to the north-east.

Almost unbelievably, cramped Church Cove used to be the base for a prosperous pilchard fishery. It has well-preserved courtyard fish cellars and a circular capstan house, now converted into private dwellings. The old lifeboat house was built facing across the slip, so that the boat had to be turned through 90° before being launched. The modern lifeboat station, immediately to the south of the cove, was opened in 1961 by HRH Prince Philip, the Duke of Edinburgh, who remarked: 'This is the second time that I have had a hand in launching the Duke of Cornwall', as he inaugurated the new lifeboat of that name.

AROUND THE LIZARD

In rough conditions yachts should keep about three miles south of the land, but short cuts are feasible in fair weather, provided that one is alert to the risk of overfalls where current meets swell.

Rocks extend half a mile south of the Lizard but two of the outliers, Men Hyr and the Mulvin, dry by 4.1m and 4.7m respectively, so they will often be visible, although covered at MHWS (5.3m). Neither should be approached closely and the Mulvin has a drying outlier about 50m to its west. The submerged Vrogue Rock lies about half a mile south-

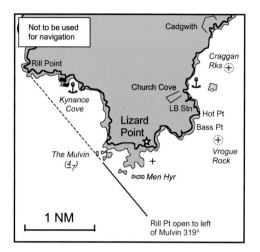

Fig 30 The Lizard.

east of Hot Point, its position indicated by pairs of beacons on the cliffs. These beacons are shown on UKHO Charts 154 and 2345.

South of the Lizard, the main tidal stream turns to the west at about HW Dover –0230, but an earlier SW-going eddy spills around Bass Point and a boat leaving Church Cove should have a fair current from about HW Dover –0400. However, this tongue of current creates early overfalls if it meets waves or swell, so it may be necessary to stand offshore to avoid broken water.

For a yacht travelling eastward from Mounts Bay, there is a possible waiting anchorage in Kynance Cove, a spectacular beauty spot between cliffs of lustrous green and red serpentine (see photo on back cover). Going ashore by dinghy is only safe when the swell is negligible but we have landed and re-embarked successfully in the protection of the foreshore rocks. Coasters used to beach in this cove, when they visited a watermill that stood in the small valley. The millstones are still there, serving as the thresholds of two cottages. South of the Lizard, the east-going stream starts at HW Dover +0315 but again there is an early eddy which runs south-east from about HW Dover +0130, when the Mulvin should be uncovered. A transit of the Mulvin on Rill Point clears all the other Lizard rocks.

Popular history paints the Cornish as a race of scheming wreckers, luring hapless ships to their doom by decoy lanterns. In reality, little luring was required, as natural forces produced wrecks in abundance, without assistance from the locals. Broken ships and their cargoes were certainly regarded as a regular and legitimate source of income, particularly on the Lizard Peninsula where there was a tradition of earning a living by rough measures, well away from the authority of central government. Despite his unconventional sources of income, Sir John Killigrew died in debt and his son searched for means of restoring the family fortunes. In 1619 he constructed a lighthouse on the Lizard, not as a philanthropic gesture but with the object of collecting light dues. The inhabitants of the area immediately protested that their traditional benefits from shipwrecks would be diminished. More significantly, dues were difficult to collect, so the light was extinguished in 1631.

MOUNTS BAY

Mounts Bay has a rotten reputation, being wide open to the Atlantic. There is only one all-tide harbour of refuge, at Newlyn, and that is principally a fishing port where yachts are politely tolerated rather than encouraged. Penzance has a secure wet basin but its opening hours are limited. In some of the minor harbours there is theoretical shelter but swell can cause a heavy surge and yachts may not be suitably equipped for bouncing off the walls. On the other hand, if the wind is light or moderate from between north and east, there are several useful anchorages where piers or harbour walls offer some chance of getting ashore in mild swell.

Mullion Cove

THIS WAS THE TRADITIONAL WAITING ANCHORAGE for ships that were bound up-Channel but delayed by an east wind. The anchorage is between Mullion Island and the shore, although the island does not provide any significant protection. A low swell is always present but if a yacht anchors in deep water, it may simply make her rise and fall gently, rather than rolling. The swell can increase without warning and the harbour must not be used as a refuge, although it is usually possible to go ashore by dinghy.

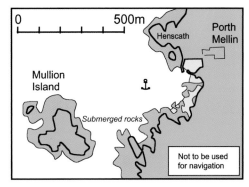

Fig 31   Mullion Cove.

Mullion is a place to relish the surroundings of deep, clear water and grand cliffs. Being here in fine weather is a privilege but do not overstay the welcome. If an onshore wind is likely, head for Newlyn or Penzance or retreat around the Lizard.

St Michael's Mount

THE HARBOUR OF ST MICHAEL'S MOUNT faces the mainland but is not immune to swell. While moored alongside the quay, even in fine weather, we have experienced a fore-and-aft surge that tended to roll our fenders off the gunwale as they rasped against the rough granite masonry. If I were caught here in a strong onshore blow, I should want to be moored in the middle of the harbour and well clear of the walls.

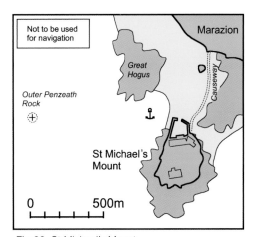

Fig 32   St Michael's Mount.

Given a gentle offshore wind, there is no need to worry about fenders or walls, as there is a deepwater anchorage just outside the harbour, between the Mount and the Great Hogus Rocks, the peaks of which are just visible at high water. The Mount is an entertaining place to explore and water is available on the quay. For provisions it is necessary to go into Marazion but one can walk along the causeway at low tide.

Lamorna Cove

IN NORTHERLY WINDS, shelter can be found under the bulge of Land's End where, of several possible cove anchorages, Lamorna is the only one with a pier. The inlet is a simple 'V' in the cliffs, with some rocks extending about 100m from the eastern side but space

St Michael's Mount. The deepwater anchorage is
between the harbour and the Great Hogus Rocks.

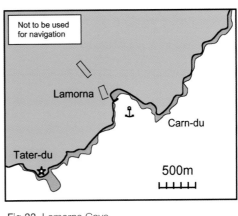

Fig 33 Lamorna Cove.

for several boats to anchor in the middle. The pier was built for shipping out quarried granite, which explains the chaotic, tumbled rocks on the side of the small valley.

Swell was always a problem and vessels that were loading stone often had to move out of the cove until it subsided. Even slight swell causes waves to break on the slip, inside the harbour, and the pier steps are in a poor state of repair, but we managed to land without too much difficulty. On shore, there are a few houses, a café and a hotel but the best known building is the inn, nicknamed 'The Wink' because, according to tradition, a wink to the landlord would be rewarded by a glass of smuggled brandy.

8 The Westcountry Rivers

When sea conditions on the south coasts of Devon and Cornwall are unpleasant for passage making or unsafe for anchoring, the long, navigable estuaries are available as alternative cruising grounds. They are even more attractive in fine weather, when the sun warms the slow-moving air in the deep valleys and it is very satisfying to take a seagoing vessel miles inland, perhaps to a remote tidal pool overhung by luxuriant trees, where the currents swirl lazily and time seems to stand still. All these waterways were once busy trading routes dotted with industrial sites, and coasters sailed right to the tidal limits. Unlike those old working craft, some modern yachts are not designed to take the ground, so their owners may be understandably reluctant to venture up the narrower, unmarked gullies. However, an enjoyable expedition can be undertaken by conning a yacht upriver to a sensible anchorage and then embarking in the tender for the more intricate part of the passage.

This chapter covers parts of six estuaries. It omits the Exe, which has very few quiet corners free of moorings, the Erme, which is private, and the Helford, where oyster beds preclude anchoring in the upper reaches. It also ignores the inland ports of Totnes, Kingsbridge and Truro, which have well-marked approaches. The Tamar once had a gated inland harbour on freshwater, at Gunnislake; it is no longer accessible but we shall get as close to it as possible.

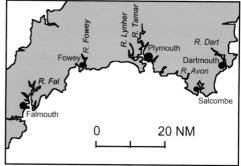

Fig 34 Westcountry rivers.

RIVER CHANNELS

Conventional river pilotage depends upon visible channel marks: buoys, beacons and stakes. Earlier sailors enjoyed fewer aids but relied more upon local knowledge. The modern yacht skipper who is a first-time visitor to an unmarked channel must manage without either. He does have the benefit of modern charts but the cartographers do not accord high priority to unfrequented waterways, so a minor gully may wander from its charted position long before a new chart is printed.

In the more obscure parts of estuaries, it is worthwhile thinking about the natural forces that shape riverbeds. Westcountry rias are flooded valleys, largely filled by alluvium through which the rivers carve channels that do not necessarily conform to the original valley shapes. Some channels can be trusted to behave predictably and we usually find deep water on the outsides of well-defined bends. Where an estuary consists of a continuous series of curving meanders, pilotage is therefore relatively straightforward. In other places, channels are fixed in position by the presence of geographical features, such as rocky promontories, which deflect the river flow and intensify the scouring action of the current. However, where the shape of the ria is a mixture of bends and straights, there will be certain reaches in which the course of the flood current is influenced by the alignment of the banks downstream, while the banks upstream direct the ebb along a different path. This usually produces double channels, with a mid-river shoal.

Where there is a wide, straight reach, the channel is free to develop meanders that are independent of the estuary form and may change its course from time to time. The interval between such changes may be decades (as on the Avon, where the principal channel immediately upstream of Bantham has moved from the south to the north bank since the early twentieth century). Channel shifts occur more rapidly in sand than in mud and Chapter 12 includes some Normandy estuaries where significant changes can occur between one season and the next.

ANCHORING

Deep pools are usually found on bends or where promontories intensify the current; they often make attractive anchorages but one should be alert to possible problems. At a few pools, the scouring effect of the current exposes bedrock and makes for poor holding. In the lower reaches of some estuaries, the scour holes and channels are very deep, requiring a long scope of cable, but swinging room may be restricted if there are moored boats nearby or if the anchorage is close to a busy fairway.

On the Westcountry rivers, MHWN is approximately 2m above chart datum and therefore, at neap tides, many places that the charts show as drying or very shallow may have enough depth for a yacht to lie afloat. Note, however, that on charts of the Tamar and Fowey rivers, the chart datum is 'stepped up' with the rising riverbed and height-of-tide calculations must be adjusted accordingly – relevant data is given on the charts.

A wind blowing along a channel will be against the current on either the flood or the ebb and will probably cause anchored boats to yaw from side to side, with the risk of collisions or dragging anchors. Whenever possible, it is better to choose an anchorage where the wind is blowing across the channel. An anchored yacht will then lie steadily, with the wind on her beam, and the force acting on the anchor should only change its direction every six hours.

In the upper reaches of estuaries, the deeper pools may be too small to float a yacht at low tide and they sometimes collect debris, such as tree branches. For taking the ground, the bed should be reasonably level and preferably of gravel. Beaching legs may be unsafe unless the bed is *definitely* firm and level, although twin-keeled craft are more tolerant of irregularities. Where the bed is uneven, it is advisable to set anchors fore-and-aft, so that the flood cannot turn the boat broadside-on to the current before she has lifted clear of any lumps on the bottom.

UNMARKED CHANNELS

Many different techniques have been proposed for navigating yachts in unmarked channels but most of them suffer from drawbacks. Continuous zigzagging, while watching the echo sounder, is more difficult than it sounds and it is easy to be led astray by tributary channels. A sounding pole or hand lead is useful but very slow. In practice, we usually adopt the channel line on the large-scale chart as a first approximation, and then proceed by conning the boat roughly by eye (eg one quarter of the river width from the port-hand bank or 50m off the starboard bank, etc). Before starting, we also pre-plot some compass bearing lines from features on the chart such as quays and buildings that should be prominent. The echo sounder is then monitored in case the channel line has been misjudged or has shifted. We expect to run aground occasionally but we allow for this by planning to complete the passage while the tide is still rising.

Good timing helps. Bricks, waterlogged tree trunks and old lumps of quarried stone lie on the beds of some rivers to surprise anyone who squeezes up a shallow channel with the very early flood. In upper reaches, banks of saltings help to indicate the general line of the channel but these may be submerged at high water, particularly during spring tides. Ideally, one should head upstream at an intermediate height of tide, giving an adequate margin of depth below the keel but with some parts of the drying banks still visible, and with sufficient remaining rise of tide to unstick the boat if she strays on to the shallows. If this all sounds like too much trouble, why not leave the parent yacht on a mooring or in a secure anchorage and use the tender to investigate the headwaters? Don't forget the picnic.

GOING ASHORE

In most of these estuaries, the foreshore is predominantly muddy. Reaching dry land at low tide may be impossible (or very sticky), unless there is an area that is scoured clean of silt. This is most likely at a rocky outcrop or at a steep beach, typically on the outside of a bend. Some of the old gravel hards, where trading barges once beached to unload, have also survived as reasonably firm low-tide landings.

Up the Dart

THE DART'S BEAUTY supports a thriving and long-established excursion boat trade, so the harbour authority discourages yachts from anchoring close to the narrower parts of the fairway. Upstream of Dartmouth, Dittisham has always been popular with yachts but there are now so many moorings that anchoring is prohibited. The nearest recognised anchorage is about half a mile to the south, at the Anchor Stone, which is marked by a port-hand beacon. River traffic must keep to the east of the beacon and yachts anchor immediately downstream. It is a short dinghy trip into Dittisham, which has a post office store, two good pubs, a water tap and even a small public shower block. On the other side of the river, Greenway Quay (landing fee 50p) gives access to the gardens of Greenway House, where there is a Tudor saluting battery hidden in the trees and a boathouse that was probably used by the young Walter Raleigh.

In moderate south-westerly winds, the Anchor Stone is well sheltered by the huge bulk of Parson's Wood. However, the anchorage has two disadvantages: it is deep (soundings of about 12m) and, close downstream of the beacon, the edge of the foreshore mud falls away very abruptly, with a rocky slope into the deep water. If a few large yachts anchor on long scopes, they leave little space for later arrivals. For anchoring in shallower water the best spot is further downstream, clear of the steep underwater slope but close to the nearest moorings. These disadvantages become apparent if the wind blows up the estuary from the south, when fluky gusts can

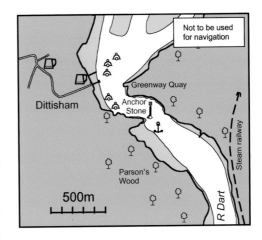

Fig 35 The Anchor Stone.

swing boats on to the shallows or into one another. Don't be put off this anchorage, because it can be a splendid place, but be prepared to move elsewhere if a strong wind backs towards south.

The next popular waterside village is Stoke Gabriel, which has some visitors' buoys but in south-west winds they are on a lee shore, which can make the mooring area decidedly choppy. At such times there is a near-perfect anchorage in the shelter of a wood on the west bank, just north of the small headland known as White Rock. Here the main channel has ample width for yachts to swing and other vessels to keep clear of them. There is no public landing place at White Rock, although some local tenders are launched from a beach slightly further south, but there are several options in nearby Bow Creek.

This tributary, which dries almost completely at low spring tides, is entered at the No. 2 port-hand buoy. There are no marks on the first bend, where old wrecks rest on the mud close to the southern shore, but it is not difficult to judge the curve by eye and echo sounder. Shoal-draught cruisers can anchor here and lie afloat at MLWN. After the next, right-hand bend, beacons mark the channel and it is possible to anchor for a few hours at

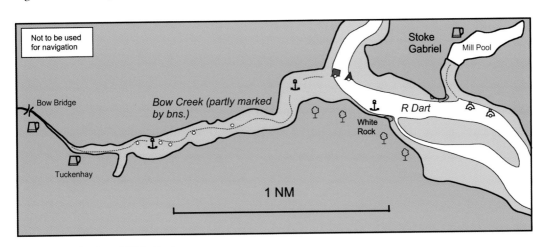

Fig 36 Bow Creek and White Rock.

high tide, immersed in the green lushness of south Devon. A footpath leads along the south shore, passing several landing places. At the hamlet of Tuckenhay, the creek narrows and the channel runs close to the south bank. There are two pubs on the creek and most cruisers can reach the first, the Maltsters Arms, which has a drying pontoon against its quay. Beyond this, the last few hundred metres of tidal water are for dinghies only. This stretch is reminiscent of the upper extremities of the Hamble and it is even necessary to float over some stepping-stones where a footpath crosses the stream. At high spring tides, it should be just possible to reach the Watermans Arms, at exquisite Bow Bridge, without the crew having to carry the tender or walk up the road.

Up the Salcombe Estuary

AT SUNNY SALCOMBE, the first anchorage of note is actually outside the estuary, in Starehole Bay. Salcombe's entrance can be dangerous in rough weather and onshore winds, particularly during the ebb and towards low water, when breakers form on the bar about half a mile south of the estuary mouth. At such times, if the wind is from the south-west, Starehole Bay makes a convenient waiting anchorage, although it is likely to be affected by swell. The wreck of the old *Herzogin Cecile* lies in the north-west corner of the bay and the best anchorage position is closer to the south-east headland, where it is possible to watch the breakers on the bar until they subside. This is quite likely to occur at the end of the ebb, although the depth over the bar may remain inadequate until the height of tide has increased.

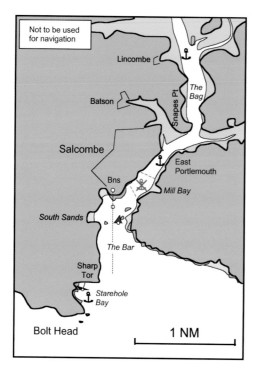

Fig 37 The Salcombe estuary anchorages.

Inside the estuary, the usual anchorage is opposite Salcombe, off the East Portlemouth shore, and we have many happy memories of lying close to that delightfully sandy beach, entertained by the constant traffic of small boats and with easy access to the town. However, the channel is aligned roughly south-west–north-east, so a south-westerly blow causes yachts to yaw violently during the ebb, and the discomfort is exacerbated by waves rolling up the fairway. The traditional storm refuge is in the Bag, which is now full of moorings, but there is an anchorage further upstream and sheltered from the south-west, off the entrance to Lincombe Creek. Foreshore mud fills the creek but drops away sharply at the edge of the channel, where depths are around 7m and there is ample swinging room.

It is possible to land at Lincombe boatyard, a friendly place where all kinds of small vessels are repaired and refurbished. The creek channel dries but the boatyard slip is accessible by dinghy at a height of tide just above MLWN. Footpaths and lanes lead into Salcombe via the picturesque hamlet of Batson, and there are good views from the National Trust paths around Snapes Point.

Up the Avon

Under the right conditions this estuary is one of the most attractive inlets on the south coast. Yachts rarely visit because the drying entrance is hazardous in heavy swell or strong onshore winds, particularly during the ebb, and the anchorages are only suitable for craft that can take the ground. However, local boats come and go on most days of the year, and Bantham was once a regular little port, busy with pilchard fishing boats and sailing coasters. In suitable conditions, the entrance is not impossibly difficult. Once inside, the visitor is well placed to waste time in the most idyllic way: messing about in boats, on a beautiful river that dries to clean sand at low tide. Worsening weather could trap a yacht inside the estuary for a few days, but I can think of no better place to be trapped.

The river mouth is about a mile east of Burgh Island. Strangers may wish to anchor off at low water, to reconnoitre the channel, and Murray's Rock could act as a useful breakwater to facilitate going ashore by tender. The best time to enter the river is shortly before high water. There may be low surf on the beach to starboard but make sure that no waves are breaking in the channel.

Devon's River Avon – the entrance narrows at low tide.

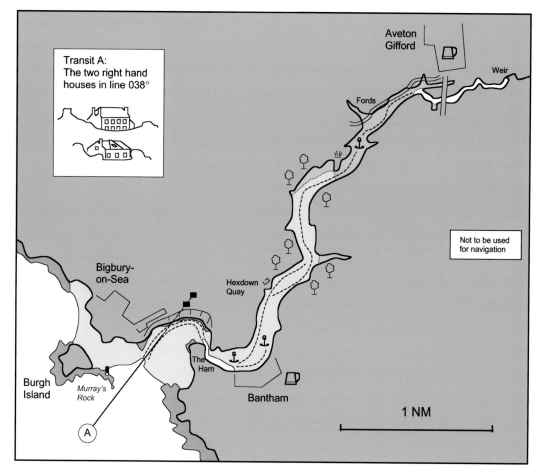

Fig 38 River Avon.

The entrance channel is fairly stable in position and the traditional approach transit is the line defined by the two right-hand houses, above the cliffs to the north of the entrance. There is no river bar but the channel bed runs steadily uphill from chart datum. As the western headland is passed, the middle of the channel lies slightly west of the transit, with its eastern edge roughly on the transit line. The beach to starboard then becomes higher, forming a steep slope at that side of the channel. On the port hand, there are some rocks and boulders close to the cliff.

The turn to the east should be started as the farther house dips below the nearer one. A short leg can be made towards a white mark, low on the cliff, but that may not be clear to a first time visitor. The object is to complete the turn with the boat pointing at the narrows, just clear of the southern headland, and the lower house approximately astern. The direct line between the lower house and the narrows is on a bearing of 143° and actually shaves the edge of the channel to starboard, where the sand has been encroaching. Take it slowly and a lookout on the bow may be able to see the edge of the submerged bank.

Just before the narrows, the channel dries by about 2m, where the stones of an old wall lie across the bed, and there is a bank to port that dries by about 3m. In the narrows very strong currents have created a deep scour hole and at low tide a long pool extends from here to the village of Bantham. The shape of the pool varies from year to year and one cannot assume that it will be available as an anchorage, as it is close to the rock face, the currents run very fast, and the sand is soft. A yacht might lie in a deep, narrow part of the pool with anchors set fore-and-aft but the consequences of the upstream anchor dragging do not bear thinking about. Visiting yachts are normally recommended to anchor and take the ground on top of the drying sand, either opposite Bantham or a short distance upstream of the village.

On the shore at Bantham, the large, thatched house is a relatively modern building but is used for the construction and repair of wooden boats. At the top of a steep path the village has a small store (summer only) and the Sloop Inn, so an enforced stay should not be unbearable.

The drying sandbanks extend well inland, with very little of the usual Westcountry mud until about two miles upstream, just short of the village of Aveton Gifford. For exploration by dinghy, the river is a little paradise and the navigable water can be followed beyond the main road bridge. It ends at a weir with a salmon ladder and the last half-mile has the character of a freshwater moorland stream, with a clean gravel bottom between grassy banks – perfect picnic territory.

Close downstream of the road bridge, a low cable crosses the river. There are also some deep pools but they are small and partly obstructed by rubble. The shallowest part of the estuary is about half a mile downstream of Aveton Gifford, where the channel dries by about 3.2m (my estimate). The bed here is firm gravel and fairly level, so this would be another suitable anchorage for a twin-keeler or a yacht with beaching legs. A minor road runs along the north bank, crossing the side creeks by fords. At low tide, it can be reached via a reasonably non-muddy route by walking across a patch of saltings.

Up the Tamar

The estuary of the river Tamar was once a major commercial waterway serving some of the world's biggest mining enterprises, but shipping activity is now confined to the vicinity of Plymouth. The busy Hamoaze reach is populated with mobile obstacles, including the Torpoint chain ferries, assorted nuclear submarines, other naval vessels and auxiliary craft, but at Saltash the hurly-burly ceases abruptly. The next long reach is characterised by wide mud banks but there are anchorages and low water landings at Cargreen and Weir Quay, just upstream of some overhead cables that might be the limit of navigation for large yachts.

This is where the real interest begins, as the river makes a huge S-bend and then leads into a deepening, narrowing valley where the scenery is on a larger scale than that of the Dart. Beyond Halton Quay, parts of the bed dry and a series of shallow patches alternate with deeper pools. The pools are generally narrow and some of them certainly shift from their charted positions, so the best yacht for these upper reaches is one that can sit comfortably on an irregular bed at low tide.

Upstream of Halton Quay, Cotehele was the home of the Edgcumbe family before they developed Mount Edgcumbe at Barn Pool. When Richard Edgcumbe forced Sir Henry

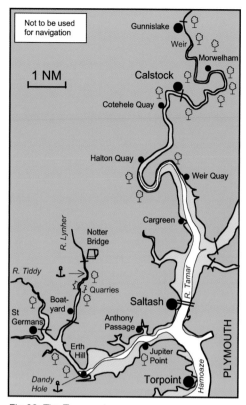

Fig 39 The Tamar estuary.

Bodrugan into exile at Gorran Haven, he was settling an old score. At an earlier stage in the Wars of the Roses, when Edgcumbe had been temporarily on the losing side, Bodrugan had chased him through his own woods at Cotehele. Edgcumbe escaped by the ruse of throwing a heavy stone into the river, followed by his cap, to divert his pursuers. To give thanks for his deliverance he subsequently constructed a small chapel, which stands on the hillside about a quarter-mile upstream of the quay. The buildings have been carefully restored; the old house is up the hill but there is a maritime museum on the quay and the Tamar sailing barge *Shamrock* is usually moored on an adjoining slip.

Calstock is the main population centre of the upper estuary. Moorings may be available by the boatyard, downstream of the town, where there is about 1m depth in some parts of the channel at low water. Above the viaduct, we were lent a mooring that was on a level patch of gravel but some nearby boats took the ground at odd angles. At this end of the town, going ashore at dead low water was impractical because the toe of the public slipway had disintegrated and most other landing points bore 'Private' notices.

Spring tides are best for a voyage to the limit of navigation. The last section of the estuary is tortuous and magnificent, winding beside precipitous hillsides where steep woods lean over the brown flood and ruined buildings can be glimpsed within the undergrowth. At one time this was an extensive industrial complex, where silver, lead, copper and arsenic were mined and shipped to all corners of the globe. At Morwelham, about two miles above Calstock, a stretch of the dock area and its equipment has now been restored and turned into a tourist attraction.

Upstream of Morwelham, the river is narrow and the scenery is even more notable where the Morwell rocks rise sheer above the water. On our last visit, we had to steer around several trees in order to safeguard our masthead equipment. At Weir Head, the old canal cut that once led through a lock and on to Gunnislake is now concealed by vegetation. There is actually a 'staircase' of three weirs, of which two cover at high water; don't make our mistake of going too far and running aground on the first one! We managed to secure a rope to a tree and warp ourselves off but I still shudder as I imagine being 'neaped' on top of a weir.

Opposite: Just downstream of Weir Head, the Tamar's limit of navigation, the Morwell Rocks rise almost sheer above the river.

Up the Lynher

THE TAMAR HAS A LONG, NAVIGABLE TRIBUTARY that is almost as dramatic as the main river. From just south of Saltash, the Lynher is readily navigable to the deep pool of Dandy Hole, south of Erth Hill, where there is space for several yachts to lie afloat. This would be a suitable place to leave a fin-keeled yacht at anchor while using the tender to venture further inland.

In the deep, tree-clad gorge alongside Erth Hill, the streams run fast and there is a mid-stream shoal. Immediately upstream, the channel runs close to the south bank and has some pools where a yacht could lie afloat at neaps, although these anchorages are narrower and shallower than the Dandy Hole. The estuary then divides, the River Tiddy leading to drying berths alongside St Germans Quay while the Lynher's channel curves off to the north and under a rail viaduct. Treluggan boatyard, or 'Boating World', has a large laying-up area on what was once a quarry spoilheap, and may be able to provide moorings for visitors. Beyond this establishment, the next half-mile of channel winds between saltings, then the valley sides close in and the river is more confined. This patch

On the River Lynher, half a mile downstream of Notter Bridge.

of countryside looks wild, with woods crowding the water. Jagged rock faces, visible through the trees, are actually quarries, which were worked until the 1930s and where the stone was loaded into Tamar barges, including the *Shamrock*. Parts of the riverbank are old quay walls, almost obliterated by undergrowth.

The next widening of the valley is totally rural, a soft basin in the hills where small fields and old flower-growing plots are jumbled with clumps of trees. The channel passes between reed beds and this is definitely the limit of navigation for masted yachts, as the trees ahead close over the river. We anchored here on a gravelly bed that was about 3.5m above chart datum, and rowed our tender upstream for another half-mile to the Notter Bridge Inn, where the river bed was about 4m above datum. MHWN is only 4.3m, so something higher than a neap tide is needed if you wish to linger for a meal. On these Westcountry rivers, spring tides are 'morning and evening' – convenient for dinner rather than lunch.

Up the Fowey

ON THE RIVER FOWEY, all commercial activity terminates at the southern end of Wiseman's Reach, as does the deep water. This upper estuary is heavily silted and its drying channels are unmarked but they lead to some fascinating places.

For a mile to the north of Wiseman's Reach, the wide bed of the estuary is mainly sand and gravel, with steep mud slopes along each shoreline. The channel doubles and wanders and it is difficult to follow the best water, but the middle banks are rather less than 2m above datum, so strangers can simply wait until they are well covered before proceeding upstream. The village of Golant once faced directly on to the river but is now separated from it by the railway, although there is a landing slip on the river side of the embankment and a low bridge under the tracks. Dinghies can pass through at about half-tide to enter a small pond, where there is a boatyard and an assortment of moored launches and other craft, close to the Fisherman's Arms.

It is possible to anchor off Golant and take the ground. However, anchoring close to the moorings could entail a risk of collision, because the local boats are likely to lift and swing to the next flood tide while a yacht with deeper

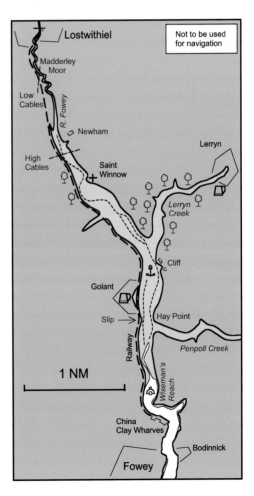

Fig 40 The upper Fowey estuary.

The drying anchorage off Cliff on the Fowey estuary, looking across the river to Golant. *London Apprentice* settled with a bows-down attitude as the ebb current in the channel scoured sand from under her keels. She might have been more comfortable on the mid-river bank.

draught is still lying with her stern downstream. A little further north, off the small settlement of Cliff, there is space to anchor on top of the mid-river banks or in the bed of the channel, which is near to the eastern shore. This can be used as a drying anchorage, or for a stop of a few hours over high tide while the crew venture further upstream in the tender.

A few cruisers are moored at the head of Lerryn Creek but first-time visitors may prefer to use their dinghy for the one-mile voyage to the village. For most of the way trees crowd the water, but there is potential for picnicking at Ethy Quay on the northern bank. This is *Wind in the Willows* territory and Fowey is generally assumed to be the 'little grey sea town', as described by Seafaring Rat in Kenneth Grahame's book. Lerryn Creek feels more like Water Rat's neighbourhood and one would not be surprised if rats, moles, badgers and even toads were peering through the branches of the dark woods, examining passing boats with interest and, in the case of Water Rat, with some expertise.

Lerryn used to hold an annual regatta in which local boats battled to be first up with the flood tide, rowing, poling and splashing to the finishing line in front of the village. The regatta was abandoned when it became overwhelmed by car-borne visitors but the River Lerryn Yacht Squadron has subsequently organised winter Seagull races, featuring not the guano-making variety of seagull but the outboard motors. The rules are simple: each boat must be propelled by Seagulls – any number of Seagulls. The committee of the yacht squadron meets at the Ship Inn, which is also a suitable destination for dinner.

From its junction with Lerryn Creek, the Fowey River's next half-mile reach is deeper on its eastern side, drying by about 2m above the general chart datum (the local chart datum steps up to follow the rising bed). The channel then forms a wide bend, its upstream end fixed by the position of the old quay at St Winnow. This serene hamlet stands on a tiny promontory, its church, farm and vicarage creating a condensed English landscape to which ramblers, photographers and artists are inexorably drawn. The quay is now dilapidated and covers at high tide, yet in the Middle Ages St Winnow was an important trading station and ships were built on the foreshore until the sixteenth century.

North of St Winnow, the riverbed rises steadily and at Lostwithiel is about 3.9m above the general chart datum. We have taken our yacht as far as Newham but, beyond that, gravel banks obstruct the narrowing channel. A few small boats are moored against a concrete retaining wall by the railway at Madderley Moor, but a low electricity cable crosses the river downstream of that point. Ascending the river by dinghy is the less stressful option! The last stretch of tidal water winds past a small park, under a rail bridge and then between waterside buildings. Just downstream of the fourteenth century road bridge, one can land at some steps or on a grassy bank, where the Globe Inn is close at hand.

Lostwithiel is a solid old town, unpretentious and displaying little regard for tourism. It was once the administrative capital of Cornwall and the principal shipping port for tin, but sand and silt from the tin streaming works clogged the river and ended that early prosperity, much to the annoyance of Edward, the Black Prince, who was Duke of Cornwall in the fourteenth century and had his local residence above the town, in Restormel Castle. When seagoing ships could no longer reach the wharves, the trade moved downstream, first to St Winnow and then to Fowey, although the discovery of local iron ore created some nineteenth century traffic in shallow-draught boats. Restormel regained some importance in the Civil War, when it was first occupied by Parliamentarians but later stormed and taken on behalf of the King. The assault may have been boosted by indignation: prior to their defeat, the Roundhead troopers had baptised one of their horses at the church font, naming it 'Charles'.

Up the Fal

AT THE NORTHERN END OF THE CARRICK ROADS, the estuary of the Fal narrows abruptly, becoming a wooded canyon. There is a popular anchorage behind Turnaware Point, although the river is deep (about 12m) and moorings or other anchored craft restrict the swinging room. Channals Creek, on the other side of the river, is protected from all winds other than south or south-west and has space for anchoring in shallower water, clear of the fairway. It is elegantly overlooked by the gardens of Trelissick House, which are owned by the National Trust and open to the public.

Two miles further on, the deep-water channel acquires a new identity as the Truro River, while the Fal itself diverges towards the east. This idyllic river, also known as Ruan Creek, is one of the most peaceful backwaters in Cornwall, although it is another place that was once filled with the bustle and smoke of commerce. It dries more or less completely, so most visitors will probably choose to explore by dinghy. There is a possible anchorage for their yachts just inside the entrance to the

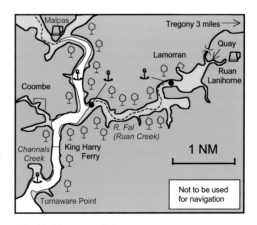

Fig 41 The upper Fal estuary.

The bridge at Ruan Lanihorne now marks the head of navigation on the River Fal. Seagoing ships once went three miles further inland to the old port of Tregony.

creek, with enough depth in the channel to lie afloat at low water neaps. If that looks too restricted, a wider alternative is on Magoty Bank about a mile to the north, where a starboard-hand buoy directs the Truro River's traffic close to the western shore and clear of the shallower anchoring area.

A few years ago we took our own yacht (drawing 1m) about two miles up Ruan Creek, to an anchorage against its northern shore and just downstream of the tiny hamlet of Lamorran, before embarking in the dinghy. In the lower reaches the channel line shown on UKHO Chart 32 was fairly accurate and at our anchorage the bed of the channel was about 2.3m above datum. Beyond Lamorran, the steep-sided, wooded valley opens out to a landscape of mellow fields and the estuary widens to become, at high tide, a very shallow sheet of water with an inscrutably curved channel – as we rowed upstream, we passed birds that were about 100m from dry land but wading on the mud. On the southern shore are the remains of several old brickworks, a reminder of relatively recent industry but now overgrown and within a nature reserve.

At the head of navigation, a country lane crosses the river on a stone bridge. Under the bridge is a weir which just covers at spring tides, but in medieval times the river was navigable for another three miles – not marginally navigable but regularly used by seagoing ships. The town of Tregony was then a major port and boasted no less than 36 alehouses, but the valley has long since silted up and been reclaimed for farming.

A little way downstream of the bridge, the Ruan River branches off through the reed beds towards the village of Ruan Lanihorne. After Tregony became inaccessible by water, Ruan Lanihorne flourished and at one time even possessed the second largest castle in Cornwall (Restormel was the largest). No trace of the structure now remains and the new port, in its turn, lost out to a steady accumulation of mine waste and agricultural silt. The Ruan River is now only a tidal ditch, although it still boasts a small stone quay close to its confluence with the Fal and complete with stone mooring bollards, where the channel bed is about 3.3m above chart datum. The village has a single alehouse, the Kings Head.

Friendly Rocks and Three-Dimensional Pilotage

9

On the south coast of England, most of the anchorages are easy to enter. If the skipper has any worries, they are more likely to relate to the weather or sea conditions than to the pilotage. To be sure, there are some off-lying rocks but if a clearance of (say) 100m is safe, then half a mile is usually safer. Around the Isles of Scilly, the Channel Islands and Northern Brittany, on the other hand, there are hundreds of outliers and large areas of detached reef, so that half-mile may lead away from a visible hazard and towards a submerged one. In many places, the most straightforward way to find a safe passage between two obstacles is to get fairly close alongside the one that is steep-to.

Conventional yacht pilotage relies to a large extent upon transits and bearings. Following a transit of two marks in line is certainly the most precise technique for inshore navigation, yet it has limitations because it only locates the yacht in one dimension, somewhere on that line. Even if a chart or pilot book shows a transit leading into the middle of an anchorage, how far can one depart from the transit to squeeze into the sheltered corner?

When exploring areas that are liberally strewn with rocks, we may as well make good use of them. Most locals do not confine themselves to transits but steer around and between natural features that they have learned to recognise. There appears to be no universally accepted label for this kind of pilotage, so I reckon the term 'friendly rocks' is as good as any. In essence, navigation based on friendly rocks employs natural outcrops as if they were cardinal beacons. They mark not safe lines but safe areas in two dimensions: particularly useful when seeking an anchorage clear of the fairway, or when proceeding under sail and tacking upwind.

Where there are reefs, banks and complicated gullies, a passage plan will usually incorporate detailed tidal predictions. Some channels are closed at low water; in other places, the natural marks are covered at high water but an intermediate height of tide will provide sufficient depth for a boat to pass them when they are exposed and clearly visible. This kind of pilotage entails thinking in three dimensions.

Transits in practice

When using a transit that is shown on a chart or in a pilot book, one should always observe the actual bearing along the transit, in order to check that the marks have been correctly identified, even if a sketch of the view has been provided. One church spire can look much like another and a dark rock against a lighter background can be transformed into a light rock against a darker background if the sunlight plays tricks or if the rock becomes popular with sea birds. For that reason, the transit sketches included in this book are line diagrams only, without shading.

Please do not regard published transits with unquestioning trust. I have sailed over all the transits shown in this book but I could not be present at the lowest tide of the year, nor could I detect any submerged hazards that may have lurked close on either side. A diligent skipper should treat any published transit as a suggestion, to be checked against a large-scale chart. Even then it is as well to remember that some rocks can move, as described in Chapter 6.

Where there is no published transit, a new transit might be produced by drawing a line on the chart through two obvious features. Unfortunately what looks obvious on paper may be indistinct in the landscape, and it is impossible to be sure that a transit will 'work' until one has been there and eyeballed it. At low tide a nearby reef may be sufficiently high above the water to block the line of sight from a yacht's deck to a more distant object. For do-it-yourself transits in unfamiliar waters, it is advisable to select some alternatives in case the assumed marks are obscured or indistinct.

Compass bearings

A bearing line can be more convenient than a transit because it requires only one mark. However, bearings read from a swinging compass card, by a human observer, will always contain errors. On flat water, a good hand-bearing compass may yield readings that are accurate to plus or minus one or two degrees, but wave motion inevitably increases the swing of the card.

All navigators should practise using a hand-bearing compass under rough conditions and making an assessment of the average reading. Sometimes it is necessary to brace against the motion; in other conditions, it may be better to balance so that one's body movements do not respond to every twitch of the hull. Big swell produces the widest swings, as it causes the whole yacht to accelerate and decelerate within the earth's magnetic field. In other words, holding yourself steady cannot prevent those swings because your body is bound to move with the yacht; the only option is to observe the readings carefully. It is essential to allow a margin for errors in the averaged readings, but how much? In the past, when steering for fairly narrow gaps between

hazards, I have assumed ±5° under calm conditions and ±10° in heavy swell. However, that judgement must be made by each individual skipper/navigator.

Where it is intended that a yacht should track along a line of bearing guided by a hand-bearing compass, there is a risk of mistakes if the compass is simply pointed at the mark. When the yacht wanders off the line, the reading will change, but an arithmetical correction may require a few seconds' thought. For instance, if the bearing is intended to be 280° but has changed to 275°, should the steering correction be to port or to starboard? That may look simple but it depends on whether the mark is ahead or astern, and mistakes are easy to make when the observer is tired and the sea is rough. A safer technique is to sight the compass along the intended bearing (ie 280° in that example) and note whether it is pointing to the left or the right of the mark. The yacht is clearly on that side of the intended line and a helm correction is then likely to be intuitive.

Making friends with rocks

Some rocks are more helpful than others; the most friendly, public-spirited rocks are those that are always above water and are steep-to on at least one side. A yacht that is fairly close to such a rock, on its steep-to side, will be in safe water. Where the side of a rock drops sheer into deep water, 'fairly close' could mean a few metres; in other circumstances, it will be necessary to allow some clearance for a sloping foreshore or submerged outliers. In some places, pairs of rocks provide comparably straightforward guidance by acting as gateposts, with the best water between them.

When one is planning to enter an area of rocks and reefs, an examination of the chart will often reveal certain rocks that possess these characteristics and can be adopted as natural beacons. Unlike man-made beacons, they do not benefit from distinctive colour schemes or top marks to aid recognition. Therefore, on a first visit to a new cruising area, they must be positively identified by virtue of their positions. On a second visit everything will look more familiar and the rocks really will look like old friends.

Can we trust the charts?

How can we be sure that the side of an unfamiliar rock will really be steep-to, or that an area of open water really is free of hazards? Unless we have time to study the area at low tide before approaching it, the best source of information will probably be a large-scale chart. Unfortunately, some charts do contain errors, and I am aware of several rocks for which the charted drying heights are definitely incorrect. In certain cases the errors appear to have arisen from copying or editing mistakes when new editions of the charts were printed. In other cases the rogue rocks are among clusters of hazards and could have been overlooked by the surveyors, or they may even be 'rolling rocks' on sandbanks, as discussed in Chapter 6. However, all these inaccuracies were observed in places where large vessels do not venture and most of the locals rely on their memories rather than charts, so that minor glitches are unlikely to be reported.

Where a chart shows the face of a rock sloping directly into deep water, with no drying outliers or submerged lumps, I am inclined to regard that as a fairly reliable indication of a safe passage. Drying heights are viewed with some suspicion until they have been checked against tidal observations.

Height of tide

For pilotage among rocks and shallows, it is very helpful to prepare a daily schedule of predicted heights of tide. This could be calculated manually from Admiralty tide tables and tidal curves, or derived from appropriate computer software. On our boat, the output is a simple table showing the height of tide at hourly intervals, written on paper and kept ready to hand. The preparatory work only has to be done once and the table can then be used for quick interpolation of the predicted height, at any time during the day, without any further graph plotting or keyboard punching.

The first use of this data is in the identification of drying rocks. Even a rock that covers at high tide may serve as a useful mark when it is uncovered. By cross-referencing the chart with the table of predicted heights, the navigator will know which drying rocks should be visible at any time and, to assist identification, roughly how much of each one should be showing. Of course, the predictions are subject to inaccuracies, including those caused by meteorological effects. In practice, more significant discrepancies are likely to arise where the local tidal curve has a slightly different shape to the curve for the nearest primary port. However, the table of predicted heights can be calibrated by comparing it with observations of charted features (such as a rock of known drying height that is just awash), to check whether the tide is behaving as predicted.

The second application of the table of predicted heights is in crossing shallow areas. If a yacht is about to pass over a shoal where the chart shows a definite sounding or drying height at the shallowest point, the navigator can use the table to predict the depth at that time, or to estimate the time at which there should be enough depth to cross. If the yacht is approaching an exposed ridge and its drying height is not accurately known, an alternative method is to anchor, note the time at which the ridge covers and then wait until, according to the table, there should have been a sufficient rise of tide.

Where a reef is almost completely submerged at high water but largely dry at low water, a passage may be most convenient at an intermediate height of tide, when there is sufficient depth to float but rocks are visible to serve as marks.

The table can also be used to accumulate knowledge, or to check the chart. If a yacht is passing over an area where the chart shows no depths or drying heights (or if the depths appear to have changed), then subtracting the echo sounder reading from the predicted height of tide will provide an instant check – approximate but up-to-date. Integrated navigation in three dimensions helps a crew to become familiar with its surroundings.

Avoiding disorientation

When conning a boat among numerous lumps and bumps, it is possible to become disoriented, particularly if various features look similar. Having a chart in the cockpit can be helpful – perhaps in a polythene sleeve and weighted to prevent it blowing away. If the steering compass has a card that can be viewed from above, that will assist by continually indicating the direction of north (unlike an edge-reading bulkhead compass or a digital compass).

Friendly rocks are notably useful in poor visibility when distant marks are obscured, or if the navigator becomes doubtful about the geography ahead. Keeping station on a known rock allows time for detailed checks while ensuring that the yacht is not straying into danger. Turning to stem the tidal stream halts progress over the ground, so there should be no risk of hitting anything during the pause.

Ideally the crew should adopt roles that enable the navigator to monitor progress frequently. When Mary and I are sailing in 'difficult' waters, she often takes the helm while I concentrate on the chart and instruments.

Low tech: the mark I eyeball

Where the seawater is clear, direct visual inspection of the bottom will often provide more detailed information than the chart – at least in relatively shallow water. Submerged sand appears green in colour, the tint becoming darker with increasing depth. Rocks generally appear dark, but the dark element is weed and higher parts of a rock may be lighter if there is no weed adhering to them.

Where a strip of sand lies between rocks, it is normally at a lower level than the rocks, unless currents or wave action have created a raised sand bar, which should be noticeable if its upper edge is relatively close to the surface and therefore light in colour. Certain anchorages have deep water where a scour hole has been formed within an area of sand. However, if the deep patch appears completely dark, it is possible that the scouring action

has exposed rock, or that loose weed has collected in the hole. Either circumstance would create a risk of poor holding.

Observation of underwater features is hindered by surface reflections. Having the sun astern will often make a dramatic improvement and reflected light can also be partly eliminated by wearing polaroid sunglasses.

Hi tech: electronic position fixing

Why bother with eyeball and compass? Why not navigate everywhere with GPS?

One reason, which is particularly applicable to the narrowest and most intricate passages, is that some charts are still based on ancient surveys and may be less accurate than the GPS positions. A more philosophical justification for a hands-on policy is that computer-aided mistakes are usually more serious than ordinary mistakes. I occasionally use the GPS to check the position of our boat in the initial approach to a tricky channel but I always use a series of simple lat-and-long fixes. I am particularly reluctant to use waypoints in these circumstances because occasional human errors are inevitable. If a lat-and-long fix is plotted incorrectly, it should stand out as an anomaly. If I make a mistake in entering a waypoint, we may hit a rock before the error becomes apparent.

GPS could be a valuable aid for making a departure during darkness from an anchorage where there are no lit navigation marks. However, that is not a good excuse for entering an anchorage that may be difficult to leave, at a time when there is a good chance of an onshore wind shift.

There is another fundamental objection to placing total reliance on electronics. We go sailing in order to enjoy the exercise of traditional skills, including those of pilotage. GPS may play a supporting role but visual observation is the only way to become accustomed to new surroundings, so that the brain really understands how to avoid the bricks.

The Isles of Scilly

10

This is an excellent, compact, self-contained cruising ground but it is not quite perfect. It feels the full force of Atlantic weather and yet there is no harbour or anchorage where a visiting yacht can find 360° shelter. Low tide exposes wide expanses of drying foreshore decorated by rocks, and most of the deeper pools are open to swell. The best way to enjoy Scilly is by using the anchor, moving between anchorages to suit changes in the wind direction, and by getting to know the nooks and crannies among the islands, reefs and sandbanks.

WAVES AND SWELL

Large waves from the west wrap around the whole island group, refracted by the shoal water until they meet in a jumble on the far side, often in the vicinity of the Eastern Isles. Within the northern half of the archipelago, the many minor islands tend to disperse big swell and it is often possible to find a fairly quiet corner. The southern half has less effective protection; St Mary's Road is wide open to the west and the south-east flank adjoins deep water, with no off-lying barriers.

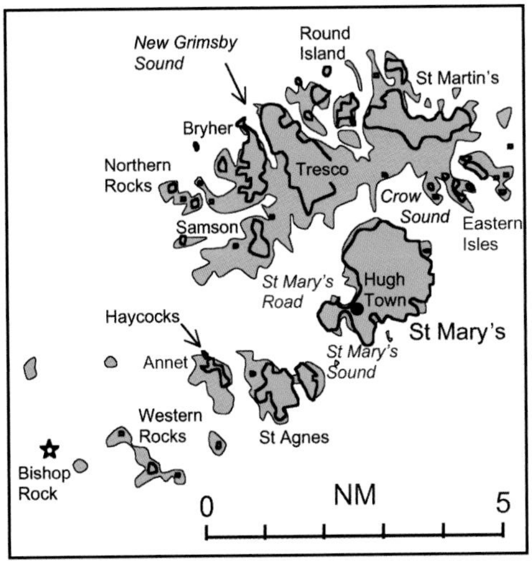

For a first visit, the best approach from the east might seem to be the big ship route, through St Mary's Sound and into Hugh Town Harbour. However, on two occasions, we have beaten up against a south-westerly wind, in unpleasant weather and with waves and swell tumbling around the islands. Under these conditions each end of St Mary's Sound can be rough, while at Hugh Town the moorings and anchorage are certainly not well sheltered. A much more civilised entry is via Crow Sound, where relatively flat water makes for a relaxed transition from passage-making to pilotage and there is an opportunity to check the chart and tidal predictions before heading across the shallows. The approach and destination should be selected according to the weather, rather than in pursuit of shore facilities or mooring buoys.

Fig 42 The Isles of Scilly.

NAVIGATION AIDS

Large-scale UKHO charts are essential. No. 34, on a scale of 1:25,000, covers the whole group and No. 883 gives more detail for the central area. The charts show a few traditional transit lines, of which the most useful are reproduced on the sketch plans in this chapter as transits A, B, C, F and G. Two extra transits, D and E, are based on my own observations. There is only a handful of man-made beacons and buoys, most of them close to St Mary's and Tresco. Fortunately, prominent geographical features are plentiful and many of these qualify as friendly rocks, being fairly easy to recognise and well positioned to serve as marks. On a first glance at the chart, the drying sand flats between Tresco and St Martin's may appear to be littered with hazards but a more positive interpretation is that they are littered with natural beacons.

TIDES AND DEPTHS

Around St Mary's and St Agnes, the principal channels and anchorages are accessible at all tides. However, among the northern islands, most waterborne traffic is confined to the high-tide period, which is when newcomers learn to find their way between the pinnacles and become accustomed to the sight of rippled sand beneath their keels. As the falling tide uncovers that sand and closes the channels, it reveals pleasing low-tide pools where boats lie in calm water, or nose on to the banks, while their crews get out the shrimping nets or set off on foot to explore the smaller islands.

Tidal constants are: MHWS 5.7, MHWN 4.3, MLWN 2.0, MLWS 0.7. During neap tides, a few of the 'drying' anchorages have sufficient depth at low water for fin-keeled cruisers to lie afloat. Nevertheless, skippers who are unwilling or unable to take the ground are greatly restricted in their options. Some of the best shelter is found in the drying anchorages and the most suitable boats for extended visits are those that possess twin keels, flat bellies or beaching legs.

SHORE FACILITIES

Visiting yachts should, if possible, arrive in Scilly with full food lockers and full tanks. An extended stay, however, is very enjoyable if you can arrange the time, and is bound to create a need for some top-ups.

Hugh Town has most of the shops and other facilities but it is busy during popular holiday periods. In bad weather, bringing supplies on board by dinghy may be a fraught business because both Hugh Town Harbour and Porth Cressa can become choppy, even when they are nominally sheltered. If a yacht is lying elsewhere, secure in a quiet and well-protected anchorage, it should not be necessary to uproot and move in order to obtain provisions, because each of the other inhabited islands – Tresco, St Martin's, Bryher and Agnes – has at least one shop that sells basic supplies and one or more establishments serving meals. There is usually a wide range of fresh produce on sale at private garden stalls, although the best items may be gone by lunchtime. Fresh water is more of a problem. Collecting it from Hugh Town quay involves payment per gallon and there is none to spare on most of the other islands. Tresco, however, has adequate supplies, with a tap on the quay at New Grimsby.

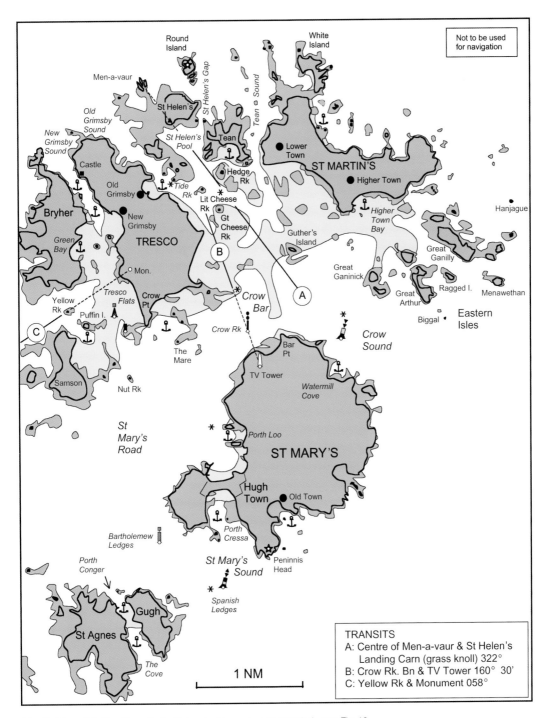

Not to be used for navigation

Round Island

White Island

Men-a-vaur

St Helen's

St Helen's Gap

Tean Sound

Old Grimsby Sound

St Helen's

St Helen's Pool

Tean

New Grimsby Sound

Castle

Old Grimsby

Tide Rk

Hedge Rk

Lit Cheese Rk

Lower Town

ST MARTIN'S

Higher Town

Hanjague

Bryher

New Grimsby

TRESCO

Gt Cheese Rk

B

Higher Town Bay

Guther's Island

Green Bay

Mon.

Tresco Flats

Crow Pt

Crow Bar

A

Great Ganinick

Great Ganilly

Ragged I.

Menawethan

Great Arthur

Biggal

Eastern Isles

Yellow Rk

Puffin I.

C

Crow Rk

Crow Sound

The Mare

Samson

Nut Rk

Bar Pt

TV Tower

Watermill Cove

St Mary's Road

Porth Loo

ST MARY'S

Hugh Town

Old Town

Bartholemew Ledges

Porth Cressa

St Mary's Sound

Peninnis Head

Porth Conger

Spanish Ledges

Gugh

St Agnes

The Cove

1 NM

TRANSITS
A: Centre of Men-a-vaur & St Helen's Landing Carn (grass knoll) 322°
B: Crow Rk. Bn & TV Tower 160° 30'
C: Yellow Rk & Monument 058°

Fig 43 Isles of Scilly – the principal islands. For a view on transit A, see Fig 46.

ANCHORAGES AROUND ST MARY'S

Much of Hugh Town Harbour is occupied by moorings and by the ferry turning area, leaving hardly any space for anchoring. There is a set of visitors' moorings but they are very closely spaced (yachts sometimes nudge against the buoys astern when the latter are not occupied) and are very popular in busy periods.

Porth Loo

PORTH LOO IS A FAIR WEATHER ANCHORAGE immediately to the north of Hugh Town Harbour, between Taylor Island and Newford Island. The approach is from due west, taking care to avoid the outlying rocks, and most boats bring up mid-way between the two islands. It is generally a very agreeable spot in easterly winds, though less so if swell is rolling in from the west, surging over the rocks and breaking on the beach. In the outer part of the anchorage, boulders on the bottom are close to the surface at low springs, although neap tides should allow enough depth to anchor further inshore.

Porth Cressa

USUALLY REGARDED AS THE OBVIOUS ALTERNATIVE to Hugh Town Harbour when the wind is from north-west, Porth Cressa must be entered between two wide reefs but there are friendly, above-water rocks on each side, close to the edges of the reefs. The best anchorage is on a fairly large patch of sand, normally visible underwater, and the best landing place is on the beach at the north of the bay.

The principal limitation of Porth Cressa is that, although it is sheltered from west, north and east, very large Atlantic waves sometimes swing around the islands and enter it from the south. A few years ago, there was a horrifying incident when an anchored yacht was caught in breaking surf. Its skipper had felt safe because the wind was blowing offshore. This kind of occurrence is only likely in strong winds or heavy swell but serves as a reminder that these outward-facing anchorages are vulnerable to wave action.

Old Town

SO, HOW ABOUT ANOTHER OUTWARD-FACING ANCHORAGE? Before the development of Hugh Town Harbour, Old Town was the capital of St Mary's. In medieval times the island was known as Ennor, this harbour was Porth Ennor, and the remains of a Norman castle still overlook the bay. Ranulf de Blancminster, who held it in 1315, had to maintain 12 armed men and pay the Crown an annual rent of six shillings and eightpence plus 300 puffins. Hugh Town became pre-eminent in about 1600 and Old Town more or less went to sleep, but it has retained one shop and one pub – puffins no longer served. St Mary's airport is on the hill above the bay but it is not Heathrow and noise is hardly an issue.

The drying harbour area has a small patch of sand surrounded by rubble and occupied by several small boat moorings, with little or no space for visitors. Weed-covered drying rocks extend across the entrance but around low water local boats come and go through a channel that is visible as a gap in the floating weed. Immediately outside the entrance there is an anchorage in depths of 2m or more, close to the north of Gull Rock. Our anchor appeared to hold well but I suspect there is some weed on the bottom, so the set should be tested before going ashore or settling down for the night. If long waves enter the bay, the steeply rising bed will probably create a very lumpy sea state around Gull Rock, so this anchorage is most suitable for periods of minimal swell.

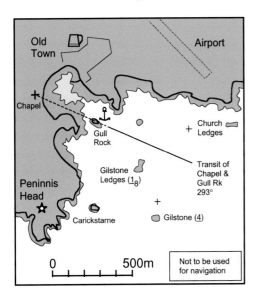

Fig 44 Old Town Bay, St Mary's.

Further out, the approaches are obstructed by several clusters of rocks, including the Gilstone, the Gilstone Ledges and other hazards about 200m off the northern shore. When entering from the south-west they can be avoided by simply using the above-water rock of Carrickstarne as a turning mark, leaving it fairly close to port and then steering for a point just to the east of Gull Rock. An approach from the east is more tricky but a transit of Gull Rock in line with a small chapel, on the west side of the harbour, leads nicely between the obstacles. I have not sketched the chapel because trees in the churchyard may grow and alter its visible outline, but the belfry should be easy to identify through binoculars. Remember to check the line on the chart, and to check the bearing.

Watermill Cove

THIS IS ONE OF THE MOST VALUABLE ANCHORAGES, offering shelter in south-westerly winds even if the usual alternative places are crowded, or are inaccessible at low tide. However, there are a few snags. The initial approach through Crow Sound is in open water but drying rocks wrap around the inner part of the cove, considerably restricting the swinging room. Here small, rounded boulders cover parts of the bottom and we have experienced our anchor hooking on to one boulder at a time, slowly wriggling across the seabed as if grappling with large ball bearings. Holding should be more reliable in deeper water, slightly outside the cove. Swell from the south-west can refract around the island and enter the anchorage from the east, when conditions might be more comfortable towards the northern tip of the island, particularly if the wind direction is close to south.

ST AGNES AND GUGH

On the western side of St Agnes, the small, drying harbour cove of Periglis has a rock-infested approach comparable with the inner part of Old Town Bay, including a low-water entrance channel marked by floating weed. Never having taken our boat in there, I am not qualified to offer guidance but I cannot resist the observation that, at low tide, the mooring area is placid, with Annet and the Western Rocks acting as breakwaters. Our next anchorage is more popular but is actually less well guarded.

Porth Conger

THE SLOT BETWEEN ST AGNES AND GUGH is divided by a shingle bar which only covers at spring tides. Porth Conger lies to the north of the bar, sheltered in winds from west, south (except when the bar is covered) and east and overlooked by the island's pub, The Turk's Head. It is a delightful place but we discovered a drawback in 1999, when the solar eclipse attracted hundreds of yachts to the Isles of Scilly. The anchorage was crowded, so we decided to anchor well inside, close to the bar, and take the ground. Conditions were calm as we touched down but, as the tide rose again, a very long, slow swell, with a height of only a few centimetres, entered the inlet. Our boat was repeatedly lifted and dropped on to the sand with a series of jarring, jangling thumps before it finally floated freely. The impacts were less serious than they sounded but were a vivid illustration of the effect of swell in a drying anchorage. At first sight, Porth Conger looks as if it is well protected but its entrance faces north-west and there are hardly any wave

Porth Conger. The permanent moorings are positioned so that boats will lie afloat at low spring tides. At neaps, the visiting yachts have been able to anchor a little further inshore without taking the ground.

breaks between there and Newfoundland. Stick to the area of deep water, which is more generous during neap tides.

The Cove

SOUTH OF THE SHINGLE BAR, the Cove has a greater area of deep water than Porth Conger. The approach is 'straight up the middle' but anchors should be laid clear of the cables that also run up the middle. Some swell motion is likely to be felt on most days but there should be no need to take the ground.

BETWEEN TRESCO, BRYHER AND SAMSON

This zone includes New Grimsby Sound, which is commonly regarded as the best deep-water anchorage in the islands. It acts as a magnet for yachts, although access to and from the south is hampered by the drying Tresco Flats.

New Grimsby

A LINE OF VISITORS' MOORING BUOYS has been laid parallel with the Tresco shore, restricting the space for anchoring but ensuring that some yachts, at least, are arranged in neat lines. There is still some room for visitors to anchor on the Bryher side, clear of local boat moorings, although it is necessary to keep clear of cables in the southern part of the Sound. Extensive patches of weed partly cover the bottom but, with care and a pair of polaroid glasses, it is possible to place the anchor on clean sand before digging it in. Further north, under Cromwell's Castle, there is greater swinging room in depths of around 10m and this is the best anchorage for large yachts, although it is nearer to the open ocean and feels less cosy (see photo on back cover).

In westerly winds, swell enters the sound from the north-west and seems to run along the Tresco shore. On our last visit, yachts on the visitors' buoys were rolling more than those anchored near to Bryher and some of them had taken advantage of an early-season lack of visitors to moor fore-and-aft between two buoys apiece, thereby lying with their sterns to the swell.

Green Bay

IF A WESTERLY WIND VEERS TO NORTH-WEST, New Grimsby becomes decidedly uncomfortable and those skippers whose boats can stand upright will be inclined to move into the drying anchorage at Green Bay. Scattered rocks lie in the southern half of this bay but there is a fairly clean area of sand in the northern part and this dries by between 1m and 2m, with the deeper berths being more affected by the tidal stream.

The anchorage in the low water pool between Puffin Island and Samson.

Puffin Island

WHEN THE SUN COMES OUT AND THE WIND GOES DOWN, this is one of the best low-water anchorages: a pool between Samson and Puffin Island with a depth of about 1m. The pool is formed by currents and wave action and, at the time of our last visit, displayed some interesting variations. The current UKHO chart indicates the anchorage to the west of Puffin Island and an isolated drying rock close to Samson. We found that the pool had migrated southward and a new group of drying rocks lay near to the UKHO anchor symbol. These were almost certainly boulders that had been shifted by big waves coming through the gap between Samson and Bryher.

To leave this anchorage at low tide, without waiting for the flats between Tresco and Samson to cover, transit C (Yellow Rock in line with monument) leads safely to open water, which can then be followed around to St Agnes or St Mary's.

Crow Point

THE RECOMMENDED TRACK ACROSS TRESCO FLATS is shown on the UKHO charts as a wide zigzag, the shallowest point of which is between Samson and Bryher and dries by approximately 1m. A yacht waiting to cross it from the south could simply anchor close to the beacons but there is also a pleasant and under-rated spot to the east of Crow Point, tucked in under the Tresco shore and with charted depths of between 0.5m and 1.0m. The pilotage marks are Nut Rock, the Mare and the above-water heads to the east of Crow Point. This is the only anchorage that is both near to Tresco and sheltered in north-west winds. From the ferry landing at Crow Point, there is a walk of about a mile to the store and inn at New Grimsby.

BETWEEN TRESCO AND TEAN

Much of the area between Tresco, Tean and St Martin's is uncovered at LAT but the parts that are used as the principal navigable channels dry by less than 1m. Therefore, when the height of tide is above about 3m, yachts can move around fairly freely. Of the assorted clumps of rock, many have heads that are always above water and visible, although some of them are rather small. When the navigator has identified these friendly rocks, it is possible to concentrate on avoiding the less cooperative half-tide ledges.

For boats crossing the flats from the south, Transit A is a good, general guideline. The triple peaks of Men-a-vaur are unmistakable although, to a first-time observer, the softer bump of St Helen's Landing Carn may appear inconspicuous unless lighting conditions produce good contrast of colour or shading. If this line is leading straight upwind but the weather is too pleasant for motoring, it is possible to dispense with the transit and tack up the fairway, assisted by the natural beacons – principally Guther's Island, Great and Little Cheese Rocks and Hedge Rock.

The best entry points from the north are Old Grimsby Sound and St Helen's Gap, between St Helen's and Tean. In Old Grimsby Sound, there are drying shoals on the northern side of the entrance but deep water on the southern side, to within about 100m of the Tresco shore. St Helen's Gap looks complicated but has distinctive gateposts, the East and West Gap Rocks, which stand on either side of the narrowest part, fairly close to the edges of the reefs.

St Helen's Pool

THIS USED TO BE A FAVOURED ANCHORAGE FOR SMALL SAILING SHIPS, being surrounded by islands and rocks but also having alternative entrances to permit arrivals and departures in most wind directions. It probably remains the best all-round anchorage for large yachts whose skippers wish to make an extended stay, without having to move for wind shifts and without any worries about swinging room. If I had a 60 footer, I should be tempted to anchor it right in the middle of this pool and go everywhere in my (no doubt large and fast) tender. For smaller yachts in poor weather, however, it can be rather a bleak and windswept place, with an unsettling, random swell at high tide when the shoals to the west are covered. The defences break up really big waves but conditions may be far from calm, and we have seen an anchored ketch, in a strong northerly wind, pitching her bowsprit into waves that were entering through St Helen's Gap.

Old Grimsby

YACHTS APPROACHING OLD GRIMSBY FROM THE SOUTH can either come up along Transit A (or close to it) and then use Little Cheese Rock as a turning mark, or via Transit B before following the Tresco shore, using echo sounder and eyeball to stay just clear of the beach. Off Old Grimsby Harbour, there are a few visitors' moorings but also space to anchor and the bottom is sandy with the usual patches of weed. The rocks to the north of the channel are well marked by their above-water heads but Tide Rock lies two-thirds of the way across and dries by 1.1m, which can be a nuisance for anyone who forgets that it is there.

At neaps, there is sufficient depth for boats of modest draught to lie afloat close to the southern headland, slightly within the shallow bay and out of the main tidal stream. This position experiences less swell than the moorings, particularly when waves are running in from the north-west and against the current. We are very fond of this anchorage; it is usually less crowded than New Grimsby, with a wonderful vista of craggy islets and even a nocturnal light show as the beam of Round Island lighthouse slants across the bulk of St Helen's. No hustle or bustle, and yet stores and other kinds of sustenance are just across the island, less

Old Grimsby Sound.

than half a mile away at New Grimsby. When the wind swings to the north, shelter is not as good as in New Grimsby Sound but an excellent alternative is close at hand.

Tean Bight

IN STIFF NORTHERLY WINDS, when yachts in Hugh Town Harbour are jumping, those in New Grimsby Sound are rolling and the ones that were lying at Old Grimsby have sailed away, the bight between Tean and Hedge Rock is as flat as a millpond. Of course, there have to be some snags. The channel between Tean and Hedge Rock has an electrical cable laid along it and the area to its north dries completely at spring tides, although twin-keelers will sit very comfortably on the central area of firm sand close to the steep shingle of the upper beach, where the water becomes tolerably warm for swimmers. At MLWN, part of that area has a depth of about 1.5m. At other times, to make good use of the channel without interfering with the cable, it is a simple matter to turn into the bight from the channel, nose slowly upwind for a few boats' lengths, then lower the anchor and drop back into the deeper water.

The anchorage in the bight to the south of Tean. The channel lies between Hedge Rock (on the right of the photograph) and the anchored yachts.

The middle of Tean is largely covered by scrubby vegetation but for anyone who fights to its summit, there is an instructive view over the complexities of the surrounding waterways. Please note that, in order to avoid disturbing nesting birds, visitors are requested not to land on the island until after 20 July. For early-season visitors who want to get ashore elsewhere to stretch their legs, the anchorage is less than half a mile from the eastern end of St Martin's. It is a short trip in the tender, with Tean providing shelter from the north for most of the way, although caution is required when crossing Tean Sound, which may be choppy.

ST MARTIN'S

Visiting St Martin's from Tean Bight makes a lot of sense because this island's own anchorages all have drawbacks. However, there is a choice to suit most wind directions if the skipper is willing to take some trouble with the pilotage.

Tean Sound

THIS GULLY HAS TO BE INCLUDED AS A POSSIBLE ANCHORAGE, since it boasts deep water and shelter from east or west. However, the best of the deep water is occupied by moorings, the currents are fairly strong and the bottom is partly rock, so I have always

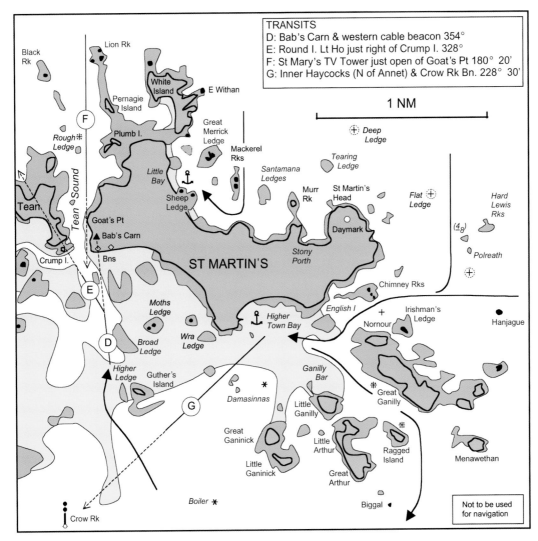

Fig 45 Around St Martin's.

been reluctant to anchor in the middle and risk snagging ground chains. At neaps and in a westerly wind, we have managed to lie close to the Tean side of the sound and just north of Crump Island, taking care to keep clear of the foreshore rocks. North of Goat's Point, there is more room but also more swell, so that position is best suited to settled conditions.

From the south, the most direct access to Tean Sound is across the drying flats. In fine weather, most people do this traverse 'by eye', because the submerged areas of rock are usually visible underwater, as black masses, and the tip of Broad Ledge makes a useful mark when it is visible. Unfortunately, although the current UKHO charts show Broad Ledge as above water at MHWS, it actually covers at a lower height of tide, about 5.1m. Therefore, to assist us at high spring tides and in overcast weather, we tested Transits D and E, as shown on the sketch plan.

When starting from south of Guther's Island, the first obstacle is Higher Ledge (dries by 4m). Its weed may be visible on the surface but one can play safe at this point by

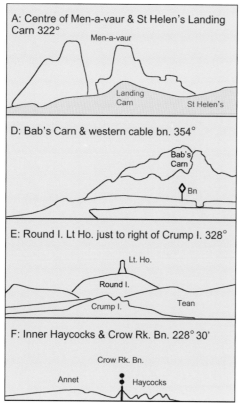

A: Centre of Men-a-vaur & St Helen's Landing Carn 322°

Men-a-vaur

Landing Carn

St Helen's

D: Bab's Carn & western cable bn. 354°

Bab's Carn

Bn

E: Round I. Lt Ho. just to right of Crump I. 328°

Lt. Ho.

Round I.

Crump I.

Tean

F: Inner Haycocks & Crow Rk. Bn. 228° 30'

Crow Rk. Bn.

Annet

Haycocks

Fig 46 Isles of Scilly – views on selected transits from Figs 43 and 45.

keeping to the west. If Broad Ledge is covered, Transit D defines the next leg. Please note that there are two cable beacons and this transit uses the left-hand one. On Bab's Carn, bushes are trying to obscure the summit but the bearing should be checked as a matter of course to make sure there is no confusion. Transit E leads between ledges drying by 3.9m and 2.5m, and then there is deep water through the middle of Tean Sound.

The northern mouth of Tean Sound, which takes us towards our next anchorage, has a line of shoals in the middle. Black Rock, close to the end of the line, is always above water but most of the others dry by between 1.4m and 2.3m. Transit F, which needs visibility of more than 3 miles, passes very near to some of the hazards and crosses a shallow spur west of Lion Rock. Fortunately, there are also some friendly rocks: on the long reef that extends from St Martin's to Lion Rock, Plumb Island, Pernagie Island and the western outlier of the Lion Rock group are all within 50m of navigable water. This useful row of natural beacons can be reassuring when a yacht is plunging over a jumble of waves and steering on the transit is tricky. Close to the south end of the transit, by Rough Ledge, it is possible to diverge a little to the east. At the north end, if swell is piling up on the shallow spur by Lion Rock, a track about half-way between the Lion Rock group and Black Rock will be in deeper water.

Little Bay

OFF THE NORTHERN COAST OF ST MARTIN'S, the deep bay between White Island and St Martin's Head offers protection from the south-west. If St Martin's were an isolated island in the Atlantic, the normal landing place or harbour would certainly be on this side. As it is, the quays and slips all face towards the neighbouring islands and this northern shore is completely undeveloped. It is guarded by seven clusters of rocks but the gaps between the clusters are fairly wide and certain rocks make convenient pilotage marks.

Atlantic swell refracts around White Island. It has least effect in the western corner of the bay but is more noticeable at the eastern end and can heap and break over the shoals to the north and east of St Martin's Head. (Please note that there are several shallow patches in this area, in addition to the rocks that are indicated on the sketch plan, Figure 45.)

Little Bay, on the north side of St Martin's.

Let's have a look into Little Bay, which is probably the best anchorage when the wind is between west and south. A yacht that is approaching from the west can enter calmer water by turning down the eastern side of White Island, the extremity of which is marked by the prominent rock stack of East Withan. The next mark is the Mackerel Rocks, which consist of two above-water rocks with drying ledges extending to their north and south. Their eastern side is steep-to and can be passed fairly close while steering due south. The simplest way to avoid their southern ledge is to continue on this course until rather more than half-way to the St Martin's cliffs, and then turn towards the west. This track then leads inshore of rocks that are covered at high tide. However, they can be avoided with the aid of Sheep Ledge, which is the next natural beacon and can be passed on its north-eastern side at a distance of (say) 100m. On either side of Little Bay, the foreshore rocks cover but will often be visible underwater against the lighter sand of the anchorage.

That approach might seem tortuous but it is straightforward at all heights of tide, a complete stranger should be able to identify the marks, and the skipper only has to concentrate on one mark at a time. Little Bay is a splendid arc of white granite sand and about 300m to the north of the beach, on a flat area of grass, there is a fascinating collection of stone mazes to entertain the crew.

Higher Town Bay

THIS ANCHORAGE DRIES, but only just, and many yachts will be able to lie afloat at MLWN. At lower tides, the main area of sand is clean, firm, almost flat and generally suitable for the use of beaching legs. While the island's all-tide ferry landing slip is in Tean

Sound, Higher Town Bay is the centre of activity for the launching and recovery of local boats and the base for the rowing gigs.

The usual track into Higher Town Bay from the south is along Transit G, passing close to the Damasinnas, which dry by 2.4m. It can also be entered from the east, between Chimney Rocks and Nornour. There are some shallow rocks in this channel but they are below chart datum (and therefore should be below a yacht's keel whenever there is sufficient depth for that yacht to enter the drying Higher Town Bay). On the south side of the channel, however, the dangerous outer rocks of Irishman's Ledge are covered at high tide. The Isle of Scilly packet *Earl of Arran* was wrecked on these in 1872. In my opinion, the simplest strategy for a stranger is to approach the Chimney Rocks from due east and then leave their outer head about 100m to starboard. If this approach is commenced from a point close to the north of the prominent stack of Hanjague, recognition of the various rocks should be reasonably straightforward.

For yachts coming around the island from the north to enter Higher Town Bay, the deepwater track lies outside Deep Ledge, Tearing Ledge and the Hard Lewis Rocks, whose names give you fair warning! However, when the western head of Polreath is uncovered

Higher Town Bay, St Martin's. To seaward of the moorings, the sand dries by about 0.4m but at low neap tides there is enough depth for most yachts to lie afloat.

– at a height of tide less than 4.8m – it is possible to take a short cut by using it as a mark and passing on its western side. Steering due south and fairly close to the western head of Polreath will keep clear of Flat Ledge, although the latter is 1.2m below chart datum and therefore should only be a hazard at low tide. This short cut should only be contemplated in light winds and slight swell because any breaking wave crests could obscure the low tip of the mark.

Once past Chimney Rocks, the next obstruction is English Island, a broad, weedy ledge that covers at MHWS. To the south of it, the best water is found approximately due west of Nornour and then the way into Higher Town Bay is clear. Further south, the sand ridge of Ganilly Bar dries by nearly 2.5m.

If Transit G's distant back mark, the inner peak of the Haycocks, is obscured by poor visibility, or if a more scenic passage to the south is required, there is an alternative and picturesque channel between Great Ganilly and Ragged Island. A couple of isolated rocks lie between the islands but charts show them as awash at chart datum, so they should be lower than the sand in Higher Town Bay.

FINAL THOUGHTS

In fine weather, the minor channels around and between the islands are very attractive, but there may be a few surprises. For instance, current UKHO charts show the brow to the east of Little Arthur as drying by 2.0m, whereas the actual drying height is approximately 5.2m (my estimate). Given sufficient rise of tide, it is possible to sail across the flats between Higher Town Bay and Tean Sound, using the above-water heads of Moths Ledge as marks and passing to the south of Wra Ledge, but the latter dries by about 4.6m (my estimate), rather than the 1.8m that is shown on the charts. That appears to have been an editing error by the cartographers, as some older charts show Wra Ledge as drying by 4.9m. In other places, such as the pool by Puffin Island, rocks really do move. Because there are numerous drying rocks, errors on charts may have gone unnoticed and one should regard every passage as being in partially uncharted waters. When the seabed is visible, it is generally a good policy to sail over light-coloured sand rather than dark-coloured rock.

Foreign Foreshores and Big Tides

11

On the southern side of the English Channel, our pilotage must take account of some additional factors. Those craggy outcrops that resemble huge tank traps are merely bits of the local geology, fashioned by Mother Nature on a bad day. However, many of the softer foreshores are covered by structures resembling small tank traps, erected by shellfish farmers. The greater rise and fall of tide complicates anchoring and makes the drying reefs more impressive but also creates temporary anchorages, some of which are useful for dodging the strong currents.

French foreshores

On the coasts of Normandy and Brittany, substantial areas of drying sand are obstructed by equipment used for oyster and mussel farming. One of the most common types of oyster bed consists of long, low trestles, fabricated from welded steel bars and supporting oysters in perforated sacks. The trestles are laid in parallel rows, fairly near to the low water mark, so they are covered for most of each tide but the flat-bottomed oyster boats or *plates* can be beached between the rows at low springs. In clear water, submerged trestles may be visible as groups of long, dark rectangles. They are usually marked by small stakes (think large twigs), which guide the oyster boats but do not provide much warning for yachts.

Some shellfish beds are maintained in low, walled enclosures and there are also individual keep tanks, or *viviers*, commonly made of concrete and most of them now disused. In a few places, a potentially serious hazard is created by *bouchots*: rows of timber or steel posts, resembling palisades up to 2m high and mainly used for mussel cultivation. Many of these too are obsolete but they are unlikely to rot away quickly.

The locations and uses of shellfish beds fluctuate from year to year but the SHOM cartographers do not attempt to keep up with the changes, merely indicating that certain zones are used for commercial exploitation. In the approaches to estuaries and harbours, the obstructions can generally be avoided by keeping to the main fairways. Within secondary channels, or when seeking a drying anchorage away from the normal mooring areas, it may be possible to inspect the bottom if the water is clear. Where there is doubt, it is advisable to make a preliminary inspection at low tide, either on foot or by binoculars.

In some estuaries and inlets, the 'sand' indicated on the charts is not all smooth, bucket-and-spade stuff but is partly covered by scattered stones and small rocks. Disciplined rows of stones, largely buried, are likely to be the foundations of old fish traps. Many of these small obstructions would not trouble a twin-keeled yacht but might puncture a craft that takes the ground on its belly. The local boats rest happily on their beaching legs but their owners have positioned the moorings carefully so that their swinging circles are on clear sand, and may also have removed some of the stones. If there are other unobstructed areas, they can usually be found by close inspection, through clear water, or by previous reconnaissance.

Reef shelter

In Brittany, it is not only commercial fishermen who make intensive use of the foreshore. At low tide the rocks are dotted with people armed with nets, buckets and boxes, all collecting lunch or dinner. There is often a high water exodus of boats from gated marinas and drying harbours, heading for the outer reefs where, at low tide, the rocks provide shelter, the boats can be moored safely and everyone can paddle around in calm water.

Low-tide shelter is equally useful for cruising yachts. Why fight against the ebb to enter an estuary when you can anchor at the mouth, protected by rocks that would otherwise be regarded as hazards, and enjoy dramatic scenery that will be concealed again within a few hours? There are also detached reefs and islands that provide scope for exploration when they are exposed. It is usual to arrive on a falling tide, with the rocks partly uncovered to flatten the sea. Calm water will assist both the navigator's concentration and the skipper's boat handling – more so if they are the same person. Where most of the rocks cover at high water, a prolonged stay may be safe but will probably be uncomfortable. Unless the weather is ideal, most people prefer to depart as the natural breakwaters begin to submerge.

Deep anchorages

Around the southern Channel Islands and much of northern Brittany, heights of spring tides are in excess of 10m. At some of the anchorages, when visiting yachts have occupied the areas close to the beach, later arrivals may have to bring up in charted depths of about 10m. Given fair weather and relatively deep water, I am usually content to lie to a scope of chain equal to no more than three times the depth but a total depth of 20m at high water still requires at least 60m of chain. A combination of chain and rope would entail an even greater scope and a correspondingly huge swinging circle.

Neap tide anchorages

Early British 'yachting' pilot books only recommended anchorages with depths of 6ft (1.8m) or more at LAT. Where the tidal range is large this is a very pessimistic limitation, and areas of drying foreshore may offer adequate depth to float at low tide, particularly during neaps when the low water level is several metres above datum.

When anchoring over foreshore sand, even if there will be sufficient depth to remain afloat, remember to check that there are no shellfish beds on the bottom. They may not represent a direct hazard to a boat that is floating above them but any oyster farmer who finds a yacht's anchor caught in his trestles must be regarded as potentially dangerous.

Western Normandy

12

The Cotentin Peninsula sits between the plain shorelines and gated harbours of the Baie de la Seine and the wilder, more intricate seascape of Brittany. Its conventional ports of call are the marinas at Carentan, St Vaast la Hougue, Cherbourg, Diélette, Carteret and Granville and the drying harbours of Barfleur and Portbail. Beyond that selection, the options are less obvious but are potentially useful for sheltering, tide dodging or even adventuring off the edge of the chart.

COTENTIN EAST

In strong westerly winds, when the waves among the Channel Islands are throwing their weight around, the coastal waters between Carentan and Barfleur offer the prospect of cruising on a flat sea. Along the 10 mile swathe of Utah Beach there are some patches of low rocks, assorted D-Day wreckage and also foreshore shellfish beds, although the drying inlet at Quineville can accommodate shoal-draught yachts of less than 9m in length. To enter, just head between the beacons on the short, rubble training walls – but only close to the top of the tide. If you anchor off Quineville at low water, perhaps to watch the land yachts in action, take great care to dig your hook well into the bottom, because a beach that is hard enough for land yachting may be hard enough to resist penetration by an anchor. We once found ourselves dragging rapidly in the direction of Le Havre when our CQR failed to hold.

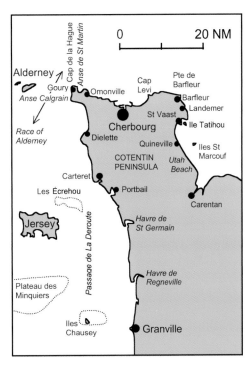

Fig 47 Western Normandy.

Iles St Marcouf

IF YOU HAVE COME TO THE EASTERN SIDE OF COTENTIN but the wind chooses to blow from the east, all the harbour entrances are dry at low water and this small island

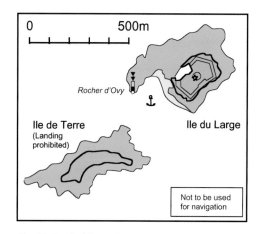

Fig 48 Iles St Marcouf.

group possesses the only sheltered anchorage in the vicinity. Locals generally visit it at low tide, when a reef between Ile du Large and the Rocher d'Ovy beacon becomes uncovered and helps to shelter a temporary cove. The outer portion of the reef, close to the beacon, dries by approximately 5.0m but the inner part is lower and only forms a complete barrier at about 3.5m above chart datum (my estimates). One can anchor well into the cove, almost to the east of the beacon, in a depth of 1.5m at LAT, where the bottom has weed patches on sand or shingle.

Landing is only permitted on Ile du Large, where a fort occupies most of the area and the outer rim of the original landmass encloses the moat and a tidal boat harbour. A footbridge used to give direct access to the fort but it has been removed. During the late eighteenth century, the uninhabited islands were occupied by the Royal Navy and adopted as an unsinkable component of their blockading squadrons. On 7 May 1797, the garrison of 500 British seamen and marines was attacked by 5000 French troops in 52 flat-bottomed boats, supported by several small warships. After several of their boats were sunk, the attackers withdrew, but the islands were returned to France at the Peace of Amiens in 1802 and construction of the present fortifications was started soon afterwards, presumably to prevent a repeat performance. A number of old guns are scattered on the beach and the anchorage is known, appropriately, as the Fosse aux Canons.

At high tide the anchorage is unprotected and often uncomfortable, with overfalls where the tidal stream flows between the islands. There is access to the boat harbour when the sill is covered but the water inside the harbour is likely to be agitated at high water unless the sea is almost flat.

If that easterly wind becomes significantly stronger, the nearest bolthole is St Vaast, although the harbour entrance is closed at low tide. When the wind is from north of east, it is usually possible to anchor in reasonable shelter outside St Vaast, behind the reefs south of Ile Tatihou, while waiting for the gate to open.

Landemer

BETWEEN ST VAAST AND BARFLEUR, the low rocky coast is reminiscent of Brittany but there are hardly any well-defined inlets and the seawater is often silty, causing poor underwater visibility and discouraging inshore exploration. The cove at Landemer has a reasonably straightforward entrance, however, and the foreshore rocks enhance the protection from south-west and north-west.

The white masonry beacon of Le Moulard, which stands about 500m north of Landemer, may assist a stranger to find the cove but is of no help for entering it. When we called in there, we took care to identify the low Pointe de Landemer and then started our approach by tracking directly towards it on a bearing of 270°. As Le Moulard beacon bore due north, we diverged slightly to the south to clear the foreshore rocks, and finally anchored south of the point. At springs this position dries and it will be necessary to anchor slightly further out. Entry is most convenient when the tide is low so that the foreshore rocks are exposed to view.

COTENTIN NORTH

Off both Pointe de Barfleur and Cap de la Hague, tidal currents are fierce. If stream and wind are together, fighting them is fairly pointless, but a matched pair of waiting anchorages is close at hand.

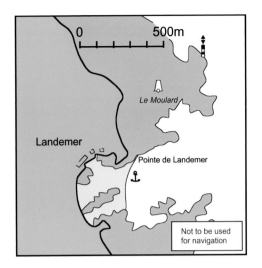

Fig 49 Landemer.

Anse du Cap Lévi

THE MOUTH OF THE SMALL HARBOUR at Port Lévi faces west and most of the local boats are moored fore-and-aft, clear of the walls – fair indication that the basin offers no real shelter for yachts when the wind comes onshore. In easterly winds, however, the Anse du Cap Lévi makes a convenient anchorage for awaiting an east-going tide. The strip of sand that leads into the harbour, between the foreshore rocks, is fairly narrow and serves as an anchorage for keep boxes. These may be tethered on very long lines, so it is advisable to anchor to seaward of all floating objects. The only facilities are peace and quiet.

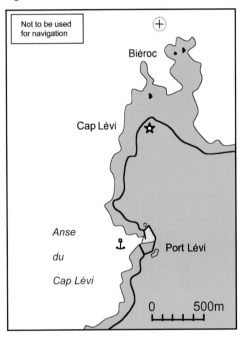

Fig 50 Anse du Cap Lévi.

Anse de St Martin

THIS, THE OTHER ANCHORAGE OF THE MATCHED PAIR, is sheltered from the west and ideally located for boats bound in that direction, down the Alderney Race. The textbook strategy for approaching the Alderney Race, from Cherbourg, is to set off while the tide is flowing east, taking advantage of the west-flowing eddy that develops close to the shore, and arriving off Cap de la Hague just as the main tide is turning. When both

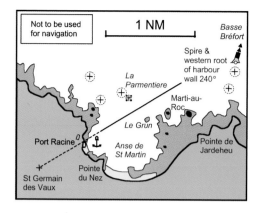

Fig 51 Anse de St Martin.

the tide and the wind are coming from the west, however, the eddy becomes rougher than the main tidal stream because it absorbs much of the latter's wave energy. Overfalls north of Pointe de Jardeheu can be particularly vicious. Indeed, this is the only place where the sea has ever managed to force its way into our port quarterberth. We were close inside the outer boundary of the eddy, where the water was slow moving. Waves that had been riding eastwards on the main stream were compressed as they crossed into the eddy, rearing into random, unstable crests.

To shorten the distance or to await quieter conditions, yachts may pause at Omonville but its anchoring area is in the tide and close to rocks, swell often enters the harbour and the visitors' mooring buoys are big, clunky things that have an aversion to varnished rubbing strakes. I believe that the inner part of the Anse de St Martin, outside Port Racine, is subject to less swell than Omonville and there is ample space for anchoring.

The charts show two drying rocks close to the middle of the Anse de St Martin but they are only dangerous at fairly low heights of tide. For boats coming from the east the

Anse de St Martin – the anchorage outside Port Racine. The harbour wall can just be seen, towards the lower right hand corner of the photo.

principal hazard is Le Grun, which dries by 1.3m. The transit shown in Figure 51, which leads past Le Grun and straight into the anchorage, can best be identified from a position close to the west of the Basse Bréfort buoy. The harbour wall may appear to merge with the land in hazy weather but should be seen slightly to the left of a prominent house with a row of dormer windows, which stands close to the north of the harbour. If the overfalls are misbehaving in the vicinity of the buoy, I would suggest continuing about a mile to the west and then sailing south, towards the above-water stack of Marti-au-Roc, before turning on to the transit. Take care not to be swept past the bay by the strong currents.

The harbour itself is even smaller and more crowded than Port Lévi. Don't even think of mooring inside but anchor about 200m to the east on clean sand and clear of the group of moorings.

In the western half of the bay, La Parmentière is awash at LAT but a departure towards the west is most likely to be made at about two hours after local high water, in order to pass Cap de la Hague just as the stream is turning. At that time, there should be ample depth over La Parmentière. For additional reassurance, it is possible to use a back bearing of 187° on Pointe du Nez to sail between La Parmentière and the western foreshore rocks.

CAP DE LA HAGUE TO ILES CHAUSEY

On the chart this coast looks really bad: facing the prevailing winds, with some of its drying foreshores extending more than two miles to seaward and all the harbour entrances either closed or very shallow at low tide. It is also exposed to Atlantic swell, which can be impressive. While sailing in a depth of 10m a mile offshore, we have observed the rise and fall of our hull being accentuated as the waves react to the shelving seabed and the incoming swell gradually becomes steeper and more prominent, each wave rolling shoreward and curling into a milky green crest before hitting the beach with a WHOOMP. Don't be unreasonably deterred, because plenty of local boats use these waters without suffering destruction. The secret is to come here when the wind is easterly, or very light, and when the sea is flat.

Anse Calgrain

BOATS THAT ARE BOUND THROUGH THE ALDERNEY RACE, towards the north-east, often start their passages from Guernsey, Diélette or Alderney. In an easterly wind, departure from Guernsey with a favourable stream will probably mean passing Cap de la Hague when the race is at its roughest. From Diélette, it is possible to arrive at La Hague just as the tide turns to the northward, but only after fighting some earlier south-going current. From Alderney, one can avoid the race by heading clear to the north of it, but that easterly wind (particularly if it is from north of east) could make Alderney's Braye Harbour very uncomfortable during the waiting period. What we need is a waiting anchorage that is sheltered from the east and close to La Hague. Goury is one option but has only limited anchoring space, immediately outside the harbour and often cluttered by keep boxes and pot buoys. The harbour itself dries at inconvenient times and a boat that

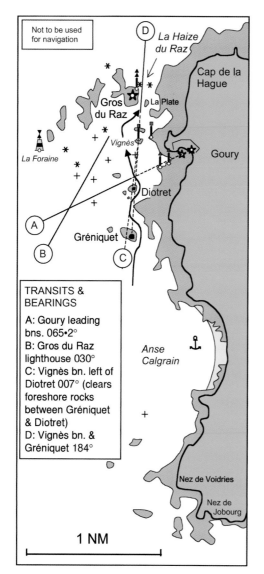

Not to be used for navigation

D La Haize du Raz

Cap de la Hague

Gros du Raz
La Plate

Vignès
Goury

La Foraine

A

Diotret

Gréniquet

B
C

TRANSITS & BEARINGS

A: Goury leading bns. 065•2°
B: Gros du Raz lighthouse 030°
C: Vignès bn. left of Diotret 007° (clears foreshore rocks between Gréniquet & Diotret)
D: Vignès bn. & Gréniquet 184°

Anse Calgrain

Nez de Voidries

Nez de Jobourg

1 NM

Fig 52 Anse Calgrain and La Haize du Raz.

is moored inside may be hard aground when the time comes to catch the first of the north-flowing tide.

A mile south of Goury, Anse Calgrain is much more satisfactory, with lots of swinging room and a clean, sandy bottom. To the south of the bay there are drying rocks and shallow patches to be avoided off the Nez de Voidries. The best anchoring position is roughly off the middle of the beach, where there is an undulating shelf of sand at a depth of about 1m and the bed then drops away to about 7m. The shelf should be satisfactory at neap tides and in the absence of swell but the deeper area is advisable at springs.

When we stopped here in a fresh north-east wind, the shelter was good and the bay was calm while the tide was flowing north. Reversal of the current induced a noticeable increase in motion, as the south-going stream brought waves around Cap de la Hague from the north-east. The anchorage remained fairly comfortable and, despite the very strong streams a mile offshore, currents in the bay were weak.

Immediately west of Cap de la Hague rocks extend more than a mile from the coast, beyond the Gros du Raz lighthouse to La Foraine beacon. The tide roars past at up to 10 knots and turns to the north at about 3 hours before local high water. Immediately inshore of the lighthouse is a 60m wide channel, La Haize du Raz, where currents are much weaker and turn about an hour earlier. This is a valuable short cut because it is possible to get past La Hague and into open water before the north-going stream has had a chance to create overfalls.

Between Anse Calgrain and Goury, rocks extend about half a mile from the land. The most notable are Gréniquet and Diotret, each of which can be used as a pilotage mark. To reach La Haize du Raz from Anse Calgrain, one option is to go around the rocks before returning towards the shore, as shown in Figure 52, via Line A or B. An alternative track is a zigzag, inside Gréniquet and Diotret and outside the foreshore rocks that intrude between them. Line C clears those foreshore rocks. Both Gréniquet and Diotret are steep-sided but there are drying lumps south-west of Diotret. This route is easier than it sounds but requires the large-scale SHOM chart, on a scale of 1:10,000.

From a position in front of Goury, one must next track 100m to the west of the Vignès beacon, to clear the drying rocks that lie around the beacon and 150m to the north of it. When about half-way between the beacon and the lighthouse, line up for the passage through La Haize. On our last visit we tested Line D, a transit of Vignès beacon and Gréniquet, which led us safely through. However, La Plate rock, on the inshore side of La Haize, dries by 5.4m and can be very helpful. If the passage is made at 4 hours before local high water (about an hour before the main tide turns), La Plate should be exposed and it is then a simple matter to steer for the middle of the gap.

Please note that there are a large number of drying and submerged rocks in this small area of sea. In particular, several rocks are below chart datum but are sufficiently shallow to be hazardous at very low spring tides. Two of them lie right in the narrowest part of La Haize, close to the north-east of the lighthouse, and there are some others to the north and south. At 4 hours before local high water they should all be adequately covered for most yachts to pass but take special care if using this short cut at low water.

It has been reported that when the wind is from the west, the breakwater effect of the Alderney Race tends to protect the approaches to Goury. Nevertheless, this remains a violent neighbourhood; La Foraine beacon lay wrecked on the seabed for several years and, at the time of our last visit, Vignès beacon had lost its topmark. Be sure to identify each mark properly, in case its appearance has been forcibly altered.

Havre de St Germain

THIS REMARKABLE INLET may be the least popular estuary in France. When we sailed in, we found only three moored boats, looking rather lonely on a square mile of sand. It is evident that strong westerly winds or heavy swell would make the entrance dangerous. The foreshore dries by more than a mile to seaward of the entrance and the only mark is Le Cabot, an isolated danger mark that sprouts from a sandbank. Somewhere underneath it there may well be a rock, but the charts also show clutches of rocks to the south and south-west of the beacon, drying by up to 6.4m. Most of these were buried when we inspected the entrance at low water, which indicates that the sand levels change from time to time. Rocks were definitely visible to the north and west of Le Cabot – ragged slabs that looked like eroded limestone – but these do not obstruct an approach from WSW.

At the time of our visit, the sand around Le Cabot dried by approximately 7.5m. We entered by passing about 50m to its north in slightly deeper water, where we later observed that there was a wide gully. The main channel, to the south of the entrance, is deeper and curves close to the dunes. Half a mile south of the entrance, it spills out over the foreshore and becomes less clearly defined. On our departure we tried to follow this channel with the aid of our echo sounder but lost the line and found ourselves crossing sand that dried by about 8m. Slightly further south, a distinct spit extends from the shore.

Inside the entrance, current charts omit half the harbour and provide no useful guidance but a comparison of various old charts and terrestrial maps suggests that the position of the main channel may alternate between the middle of the harbour and the western side. At the time of our visit, there was a shallow channel close to the western shore, which dried by about 8.5m. The main channel meandered through the middle and

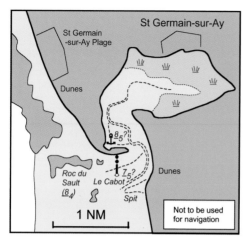

Fig 53 Havre de St Germain.

was about a metre lower. MHWS is 11.5m and the flood starts to spill into the estuary at half-tide, when the sea level is rising by about 4 centimetres per minute, so it rapidly becomes a torrent, churning up the channel and creating standing waves until the depth has increased and the harbour can calm down again. We anchored in the shallower, western channel, and were happy to be clear of the turmoil.

We had been nervous about swell, which had been fairly heavy about 48 hours earlier. However, our arrival and departure were on flat water. Spring tides gave us an adequate margin of depth over the banks, during a period when swell was slight. MHWN is only 8.8m, so there is little point in trying to enter this harbour at neaps.

Once inside, what do you get? Lots of sand, with dunes to add variety. This estuary is certainly 'different' and could even be described as exclusive. There may be some activity in St Germain-sur-Ay but we did not stay long enough to check, because there was a forecast of westerly winds and we wished to avoid becoming trapped inside the estuary.

Havre de St Germain, viewed from the entrance. The main channel is on the right and the two boats are in the secondary channel, close to the western shore.

Havre de Regneville

ONCE UPON A TIME THIS ESTUARY'S CHANNEL resembled that at St Germain, carving a mile-long bend through the sand to the south of the entrance. It was supposedly buoyed but the buoys were notorious for their absence. Some discipline has been instilled by the construction of a rock training wall that extends partly across the entrance from the eastern shore and fixes the channel at that point. Outside the harbour, there is no longer a distinct channel; at low tide, the river water simply spills across the foreshore in a broad sheet. A mile to the west of Pointe d'Agon, there is an area of *bouchots*, used for mussel cultivation, and a large mass of foreshore rocks topped by Le Ronquet beacon (beyond the edge of the sketch plan). The harbour should be approached from the south-west, where a starboard-hand buoy serves as an outer mark. There are some shellfish farming structures under this approach but they appear to be lower than the level of the channel bed at the entrance.

Inside the harbour, the main channel used to lie close behind Pointe d'Agon, where there are still some moorings and a jetty. The new training wall caused the channel to shift towards the middle of the harbour and it may take some time to stabilise on a new alignment. At night there is a light on Pointe d'Agon and a directional light in Regneville, with its white sector leading close to the end of the training wall, but inside the harbour, by night or by day, a stranger is unlikely to be able to find the channel unless it has previously been reconnoitred at low tide. This will be difficult to accomplish from a yacht anchored offshore because the beach dries for two miles from the entrance.

We decided to anchor close inside the entrance, about 300m north of the training wall, where we could be reasonably certain that the channel would lie close to the eastern shore. Our boat settled on fairly soft sand and later re-floated without problems, although the currents were fairly strong, particularly while the first of the flood was sweeping into the harbour. The channel bed was nearly 8m above chart datum. (MHWS is 11.8m and MHWN is 9.0m.)

From this position it was possible to explore on foot at low tide. Further up the harbour there are areas of salt marsh that only cover on high spring tides. From Regneville, a track leads north-westwards across the marsh to a slipway and a drying pontoon in the channel. In this vicinity, the sand of the harbour bed is muddy but the channel is fairly wide, drying by about 8.5m, with a group of moorings and some space for anchoring. Not far away, some sandbanks are much higher and there is a real risk that a stranger could take a wrong turning, run aground and become neaped. A preliminary reconnaissance of the upper reaches of the harbour is therefore strongly recommended.

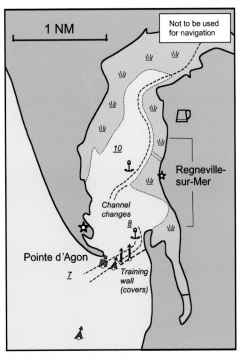

Fig 54 Havre de Regneville.

Regneville is very sleepy. We found one small, scruffy shop but there was also an excellent establishment at the north end of town, Le Jules Gomme's Restaurant, Creperie and Pub, with bitter on draught!

ILES CHAUSEY

Chausey resembles the big reefs of Brittany and the Channel Islands, but is included in this chapter because it is closely associated with Granville and sometimes seems to be joined to the mainland by a continuous stream of small boats. Most of the locals head out of harbour on the ebb, anchor between the rocks and sandbanks at low tide, and then return home with the flood. Visiting yachts – British yachts, at least – usually concentrate in the Chausey Sound, where some mooring buoys are available for visitors. Close to Grande Ile, the Sound is the only place to offer half-reasonable protection from strong west winds, and yet the real flavour of Chausey is to be found away from the crowds, among those rocks and sandbanks.

We have only visited Chausey on a few occasions and therefore cannot claim any specialist local knowledge. Nevertheless, having observed the locals in action, I should like to suggest a couple of ways of exploring the nooks and crannies. The first essential is the large scale SHOM chart, on a scale of 1:15,000. Nature reserve restrictions now apply to the area east of Grande Ile; I understand that access is prohibited until 30 June in each year, but it may be advisable to make a prior visit to Grande Ile or Granville in order to check the latest details.

The oval mass of the Iles Chausey is tilted upward towards its western side. In the eastern half most of the sand remains covered at neap tides and only limited areas uncover at MLWS. There are also extensive areas of *bouchots* to surprise the unwary visitor. The most

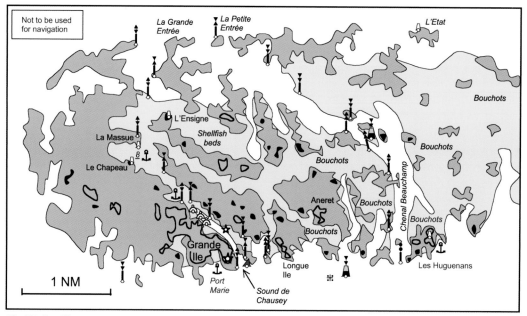

Fig 55 Iles Chausey.

Iles Chausey – the drying anchorage is sheltered by a high sand bar, close to La Massue beacon. It is important to anchor on clean sand, clear of any obstructions!

interesting parts of the archipelago appear to be the small islands on its southern rim and the mass of banks, rocks and islets north of Grande Ile. The southern islands are adjacent to deep water, with places for fin-keeled yachts to lie afloat, and the area north of Grande Ile is generally more suitable for boats that can take the ground, although there are pools with anchoring depths at neaps.

We have used the low water cove south-east of Les Huguenans as a waiting anchorage for entering Granville. There was a stiff sea breeze from the north-west and the prospect of lying hove-to off the town while waiting for the harbour to fill did not appeal. In the lee of Les Huguenans, the water was flat, the sun was hot and delightful, golden sand bars enhanced the shelter. Comparable anchorages are found to the west of Les Huguenans but rocks lie in some of the deeper channels and there are *bouchots* to the south and east of Aneret. I would be inclined to make an initial visit to a straightforward anchorage, such as at Les Huguenans or close to Longue Ile, then make a low-tide reconnaissance of the inner leads in preparation for a second, more adventurous incursion at a later date. These spots are at their best in a northerly wind, which will often accompany fine weather. Another deep-water anchorage, sheltered from the north, can be found in Port Marie to the south of Grande Ile. Take care when arriving here at high tide, because the foreshore rocks on the western side of the beach rise very steeply and it would be easy to anchor too close to the granite.

North of Grande Ile, a reconnaissance is equally valuable, but anchorages may not be obvious on the chart. Close to the northern end of the island, Chausey Sound widens to a basin of silty sand (with two or three small rocks that are shown on the SHOM chart), which dries by between 1m and 3m but has enough depth for several yachts to float at MLWN of 4.9m. This also makes a reasonable drying anchorage at springs, although the higher rocks and small islands provide only partial protection at high water.

Further north, a sand spit extends from La Massue beacon towards Le Chapeau and parts of it dry by about 8m. As the spit uncovers, it gives protection from the west and we have beached our boat in shelter on its eastern side. The bottom was mainly clean, rippled sand over a large area, but there were a few obstructions, including a large diesel engine that was still attached to the lower timbers of a wreck. Looking down through the fairly clear water, we were able to check for a safe space before anchoring. From this position, it is possible to stroll around the higher part of the reef for several hours before it is time for lift off. In fine weather there may be masts sprouting above the scenery in the most unlikely places, where the local experts have anchored in their favourite gullies between the huge rocks.

13 Half Civilised: Life at Anchor

It is possible to enjoy an extended cruise within the western English Channel without ever mooring to a marina pontoon or even visiting a large town. This is not primitive living but escaping from the crowds. On our boat, *London Apprentice*, the fittings and equipment are fairly simple but are designed to enable us to be largely independent of conventional harbours, so that we can be equally secure and comfortable in the Solent, Brittany or the Outer Hebrides. For people who sail in areas with few leisure facilities, this approach to the selection of cruising gear is entirely normal.

Feeding and watering

In the western Channel there is a choice of coastal and inland anchorages to suit most wind directions and, despite the onward march of out-of-town supermarkets, there are sufficient small local shops for regular re-provisioning.

It is also possible to top up freshwater tanks without calling at major harbours. We carry most of our on-board supply in a single tank but also load 40 litres (approximately 9 gallons) in rigid portable containers, as a reserve supply, and stow collapsible containers for another 30 litres (6 gallons). The collapsible containers are normally put in the tender whenever we go ashore from an anchorage. If there is a tap near to the landing place, one filling will provide sufficient water for at least one day.

Our general policy is to top up little and often. However, if we go for several days before finding a tap, the rigid containers are emptied into the main tank and the dinghy can then collect 70 litres (15 gallons) in a single trip. This might sound time-consuming but it is much quicker than making a diversion of several miles from the preferred cruising track in order to find a berth adjacent to a hosepipe, possibly with a queue of several boats waiting to use it.

Going ashore

The tender is an important component of life at anchor and there is a lot to be said for choosing one that is a satisfactory boat in its own right, rather than merely a load-carrying raft. It should not be necessary to put up with wet bums or wet baggage on every trip to or from the shore. The growth of water taxi services in major harbours is arguably attributable to the inadequacies of modern tenders. Proper seating and a spray-shedding hull shape make for comfort and confidence, both of which are desirable in exposed anchorages or on extended river expeditions. If a yacht is equipped with a well-designed dinghy, its use becomes a source of pleasure rather than a damp inconvenience.

Many of the yacht owners who habitually cruise from anchorage to anchorage have taken to suspending their tenders from stern davits or gantry frames. This kind of arrangement might not be suitable for ocean crossings or proof against knockdowns but it appears to be more than adequate for coastal cruising. It enables the crew to go ashore at the drop of a hat, without any need to inflate and deflate a dinghy, and it also allows the yacht to carry a rigid or semi-rigid tender. We use a comparable system on board *London Apprentice*, our tender being slung from a tilting davit frame. The dinghy has a shallow, rigid pontoon hull, incorporating buoyancy tanks, and its sides are synthetic canvas secured to a laminated gunwale. It has some of the qualities of a small RIB, but with the buoyancy in the rigid hull rather than in the flexible sides. On passage, it stows immediately above the yacht's pushpit with its sides collapsed, and does not appear to create significant windage. Raising the gunwale increases the hull freeboard and launching takes about a minute. Being able to go ashore without lengthy preparations encourages us to do so frequently, whereas the prospect of inflating, sponging out and later deflating a wet bundle of rubber might persuade us to stay on board.

A tender also offers scope for entertainment and a dinghy with decent oars and firm rowlocks will allow children to learn to row properly. A sailing rig provides hours of fun, although it may become so popular that the tender is unavailable for the mundane business of ship-to-shore transport. When our daughters were young we always carried a second, collapsible dinghy, so that the junior half of the crew could go off and play 'Swallows and Amazons' while the main tender remained available as a ferry or rescue craft. The girls became very competent very quickly and never did need rescuing.

Our dinghy has a rowlock fitting on its stern. This permits enthusiasts to practise single-oar sculling but its main purpose is to act as a kedge fairlead. I once lifted an anchor, using a dinghy that had no suitable fairlead, and was compelled to steady the chain on the gunwale by gripping it between my bare toes. That kind of experience concentrates the mind wonderfully and each of our subsequent tenders has been properly equipped to act as a small mooring barge.

Light and heat

At anchor, shore power is obviously unavailable, so it is a good idea to fit a passive charging system: either a wind generator or solar panels. Either type avoids having to disturb the peace by running a motor for charging. The panels may be more appropriate for summer days and sheltered anchorages;

they certainly appear to be reasonably reliable and we have experienced only one failure in 16 years. Solar panels are most effective when installed as multiple units and connected in parallel. If a single large panel is partly shaded or inclined away from the sun, so that its output voltage drops below the battery voltage, charging will stop. If one of a pair of panels is shaded, there is a good chance that its partner is still producing sufficient voltage to charge the battery, though at a reduced rate.

The oil lamp is a luxury that civilisation has almost forgotten, yet the golden gleam from a burning wick is immensely satisfying; a visual catalyst that enhances many other pleasures. As the setting sun dips below the horizon and dew begins to form on brightwork, a cabin lit by that warm glow of flame is so much more welcoming than one illuminated by cold amps. To be realistic, most people would supplement oil with electricity, particularly when reading, but wick lamps provide heat as well as light and the 'warm glow' is just that. For summer cruising we have never felt the need for a stove or central heating system, because our two oil lamps both have 25mm wicks and their heat output makes a noticeable difference to comfort on cool evenings. Unlike a stove, an oil lamp has no external flue and it is necessary to leave hatches partly open for ventilation, but the radiant heat alone is sufficient to 'take off the chill' and we sometimes leave one alight during night passages, so that the cabin remains cosy and dry. The lamps are very easy to maintain (ie wash the glass and polish the brass), which is more than can be said for some yacht heaters.

Overnight

Evening is a time for appreciating simple sensations. The chuckle of current against the hull and the hiss from waves on the beach seem to be more prominent as the light fades. Shore lights, flickering on the water, become picturesque at a distance but, for a really high-class treat, we need to find somewhere remote from habitation, so that the Milky Way can stretch right across a dark, clear sky. There an anchored yacht will be floating among the galaxies and the rest of civilisation, for all its luxuries, will be unwelcome.

Peaceful evenings are not necessarily followed by tranquil nights and there is always some risk that a partly sheltered anchorage will have to be evacuated during the hours of darkness. As I noted in the Introduction, this has only happened to us twice in more than 30 years, so the risk should not be exaggerated, provided that proper consideration is given to the weather. Nevertheless, people who are new to anchoring, being more accustomed to relying on moorings, will often lie awake and uneasy, sensitive to every unfamiliar noise. Putting a member of the crew on anchor watch is one (unpopular) way of insuring against surprise, but the skipper may still be uneasy and restless if he or she has misgivings about the turmoil and discomfort of getting under way in the dark.

On a competently crewed yacht, an unplanned departure should be merely an inconvenience, but people are not at their best when awoken unexpectedly so it is advisable to make proper preparations in advance, as a matter of routine, so that no one need feel uncertain or anxious – even the skipper. There are certain items of data that I usually enter in the log so that, if my mental processes are bump-started at an unearthly hour, they have a fair chance of functioning correctly. The first entry is a course towards open water. That should enable us to get clear of any immediate hazards. The second is a summary of predicted tidal streams, together with tidal heights as discussed in Chapter 9. If a yacht is lying in one of Sark's anchorages, she might be in a 4 knot current within minutes of departure. At night the skipper risks disorientation unless he or she can anticipate the strength and direction of the stream. It also helps to know which of the off-lying shoals should be well covered, which are likely to be exposed and which may be close beneath the surface.

I once made a complete hash of tidal calculations, undertaken in a befuddled state when leaving an anchorage at 0130 hours, by transposing the times of high and low water Dover. A preliminary note in the log, entered the evening before, would have served as a check to highlight any early morning blunders.

Other precautions are mainly good seamanship: all lines properly stowed, so that no rope tails can snake overboard and into the propeller; bathing ladders inboard; crockery stowed, including mugs and glasses used during the evening; warm clothing ready to hand. If the evening wind is strong and there is any doubt over its future direction, we would normally put a precautionary reef in the mainsail. I also like to have the dinghy on board, just in case. When everything is shipshape and Bristol-fashion, we can relax and enjoy our surroundings.

The Channel Islands

14

The Channel Islands have an abundance of anchorages, many of them scenically stunning. There are only a few deepwater harbours for visiting yachts: Braye Harbour on Alderney, St Peter Port and Beaucette on Guernsey and St Helier on Jersey. Of those, Beaucette is small and Braye is open to the north-east, so the choice begins to look rather limited. Yachts that can take the ground may also moor in St Aubin (limited space), at Gorey (which is open to south and east), or even in Sark's tiny Creux Harbour (limited space and open to the south and east). It is hardly surprising that harbour overcrowding occurs in high season.

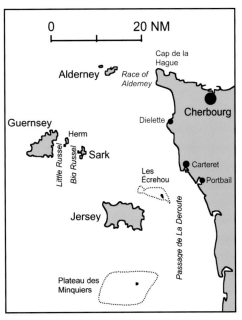

Fig 56 The Channel Islands.

Sailors with long experience of this area tend to prefer the anchorages, particularly the stunning ones. However, the islands are too widely separated to provide much in the way of mutual support against weather. Unlike the Isles of Scilly, they do not form a compact group with a central zone that is partly shielded under most conditions. A move from one anchorage to another, for shelter after a wind shift, may entail a passage across open water to another island, or an extended detour around off-lying reefs. If the wind is strong, overfalls occur between the islands and the planning of any passage, however short, must take account of the tidal streams.

The islands are also rather too small to form effective barriers against strong winds, which skip over them, or Atlantic swell, which refracts right around them. Fortunately, certain bays can be relied upon to give better-than-average protection, particularly when neap tides permit yachts to lie really close inshore.

ALDERNEY

This well-washed island has a major tidal gate on each side. South-east of Quenard Point, the current in Alderney Race can exceed 6 knots. Between Alderney and Burhou, the Swinge foams and roars at the slightest provocation. To the north-east of these antisocial elements, Braye is sheltered from the prevailing winds and is normally very welcoming,

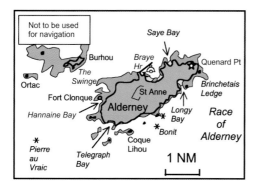

Fig 57 Alderney.

a salty passage port where long-distance cruisers pause during their voyages and a holiday harbour where families on short-distance cruisers ferry their children to the beach. Apart from the visitors' moorings, close inside the long breakwater, there is still space to anchor in the middle of the harbour. A modest charge is made but it covers the use of the showers.

Between Braye and Quenard Point, the inlet of Saye Bay is an alternative anchorage in fine weather. However, both Braye and its smaller neighbour are open to winds from the north and north-east, and then the only good shelter is on the other side of the island, beyond those tidal gates.

Longy Bay

PROTECTED FROM BETWEEN WEST AND NORTH-EAST, Longy Bay is a good waiting anchorage when eastbound through the Alderney Race. The entrance is between Raz Island and the prominent stack of Queslingue but a rock in the middle dries by 0.6m. Some publications recommend entering on a transit of the 'Nunnery' (the building that overlooks the north-west corner of the bay) in line with the left-hand edge of Fort Albert (on the other side of the island). However, charts show the rock's position as almost exactly in the middle of the gap, so I find it easier to enter by passing closer to Queslingue

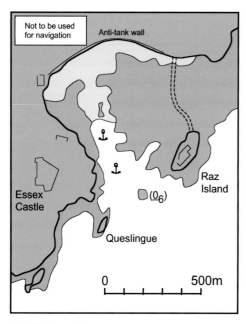

Fig 58 Longy Bay.

(say 100m off its eastern side, or at about a quarter of the distance between Queslingue and Raz Island).

The reef on the eastern side of the bay is irregular, with no features to mark its limits, but the western shore, under Essex Castle, is fairly steep-to. Visitors usually keep towards the western side, look for a space between other anchored boats and then check it with the echo sounder. In the shallower areas it should also be possible to distinguish between submerged areas of rock and sand by visual inspection. Remember those polaroid glasses and try to have the sun behind you.

While the current in the Alderney Race is flowing to the south-west, a weaker eddy develops along the southern shore of the island, running back towards the north-east. At this stage of the tide (say HW Dover +0400), an arrival at Longy should be fairly straightforward. When the main stream turns to the north-east, the current across the mouth of the bay becomes stronger and an approach must be carefully judged in order to avoid being swept past – another reason why I prefer to hug close to Queslingue.

A departure from Longy Bay can be timed to suit the first of a favourable tide. If heading towards Braye, it is better to wait until the stream has been running to the north-east for two or three hours. There will then be a fairly wide inshore current flowing northwards around Quenard Point and west towards the harbour, providing a downhill ride all the way. UKHO Chart 60, on a scale of 1:25,000, gives a good transit for avoiding Brinchetais Ledge, south-east of Quenard Point.

Telegraph Bay

THIS CLIFF-GIRT ANCHORAGE LOOKS AND SOUNDS DRAMATIC, with thousands of sea birds swooping and arguing over the crags and rocks. It also seems dramatic on the chart, apparently hemmed in by nasty reefs. Some publications recommend entering along a compass bearing to the Old Telegraph Tower, above the cliffs, but why use a compass bearing when there are two friendly rocks and a decent transit?

When approaching Alderney from the south-west, it should be easy enough to identify the Noires Putes, which are 19m and 14m high. To their north-west, the smaller rocks Orbouée and Coupé are 0.5m and 8m high respectively and there is a clean channel between the two groups. We have entered by passing close to Coupé and then following a transit of Orbouée just to the left of Coupé on 239° (see Figure 59). This track would be particularly useful when the top of Alderney and the Old Telegraph Tower are swathed in low cloud. The anchorage is surrounded by rocks (and probably some loose boulders) but is sheltered from north and north-east. Swell from the west is likely to increase at high tide.

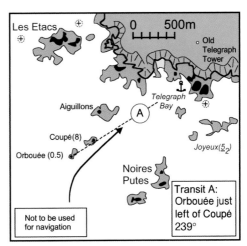

Fig 59 Telegraph Bay.

To proceed eastwards from Telegraph Bay, it is possible to make a start while the stream in the Alderney Race is unfavourable by riding the north-east-going inshore eddy as far as Longy Bay. For this passage, the easiest exit from Telegraph Bay is by backtracking towards Coupé and then passing between the Noires Putes and Joyeux, which dries by 5.2m. MHWN is 4.7m and MHWS is 6.3m, so Joyeux only covers at spring tides and near to high water.

For a passage towards the Swinge, the most straightforward exit is between Coupé and the Aiguillons, passing closer to Coupé. An alternative waiting anchorage is in Hannaine Bay, inshore of Fort Clonque. This has better shelter from east and south-east but becomes open to the north-east when the causeway to the fort is covered.

GUERNSEY

This is a four-sided island but unmarked rocks and reefs clutter its western and northern flanks. The most popular anchorages are on the eastern coast and south of St Peter Port, where shelter from westerly winds is usually adequate, if gusty, but some swell finds its way around St Martin's Point.

Havelet Bay, immediately outside St Peter Port Harbour, is close to the town's facilities and provides a free alternative to the harbour moorings or marina but can become almost as crowded in high summer. Its entrance is clearly indicated by beacons (supplemented by buoys in summer) but there are several drying ledges further inshore. These are unmarked and so anchoring positions should be chosen and checked with care. When there are lots of visiting boats, swinging room may be scarce. Fermain Bay, a little more than a mile to the south, is usually less crowded but is further from town – the one-mile walk along the cliff path feels like three miles. There are several off-lying rocks between St Peter Port and St Martin's Point, some of them unmarked.

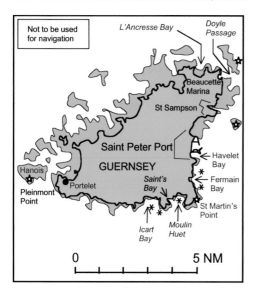

Fig 60 Guernsey.

On the southern coast deeply indented bays and coves offer shelter in northerly winds, the most popular anchorages being in Moulin Huet and Icart Bay. There is a drying rock in the middle of each, with other ledges and outliers extending from the cliffs, but sufficient unobstructed water for yachts to be conned into the quiet corners without undue difficulty. On the western side of Moulin Huet, the smaller inlet of Saint's Bay has a stone platform, perched high on the foreshore rocks, and an extremely steep slipway. An old battery is sited on the headland; its tiny magazine and the stone bed for the single gun are a reminder that coasters would once have crept in here to seek sanctuary from French privateers. Visitors who anchor here in the twenty-first century must take care to avoid an underwater cable.

These bays are likely to be at their most comfortable on a falling tide, towards low water, with swell reduced by the current as it flows to the west. It was while spending a night in Saint's Bay that I experienced my one and only mutiny. As the tide rose, swell increased markedly and by 0600 my family was in revolt. I was not set adrift in the tender, like Captain Bligh, but the crew refused to contemplate breakfast until we found a calmer anchorage.

In winds from south or east, it is necessary to look elsewhere for shelter. Some of the western and northern bays are attractive in fine weather but UKHO Chart 807 is essential. It is on a scale of 1:25,000 and shows the principal transits. Access to most of these bays entails a circuitous passage around the reefs but there are two anchorages for which the approach tracks are fairly short.

L'Ancresse Bay

WITHIN THE ISLAND GROUP OF GUERNSEY AND HERM, this is the only anchorage to combine deep water, straightforward access, and shelter from the south. It can be approached from due north, which may be convenient for a yacht that is heading south but has failed to carry its tide through the Little Russel. Alternatively, a boat coming from south or east could use the well-marked Beaucette approach channel to pass through the shoals to the east of that marina. The deep and clean-sided Doyle Passage then leads to the north of the island.

The sketch plan's Transit A may be useful for entering the bay if the tidal stream is flowing across the approach. When the wind is from west of south the best shelter is against the western shore, close to the low cliffs, in order to avoid the cable that lies about 150m off. The 2.8m drying shoal may be visible under water but can also be cleared by using Line B. The low shoreline is only a modest windbreak but the seabed is clean sand and holding is good. The western part of the bay seems to be well protected against swell from the west and the reefs to the north-west probably contribute to the break-water effect. However, moderate swell coming directly from the north-west would make the

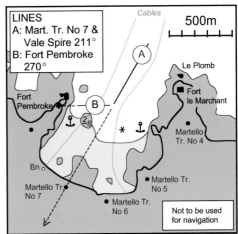

Fig 61 L'Ancresse Bay.

anchorage untenable. On shore there is a café, a freshwater tap and some splendid walks around this relatively unpopulated corner of Guernsey. Near to Fort le Marchant, a red flag will indicate that the local rifle range is in use.

In a southerly wind, L'Ancresse Bay would make a good departure anchorage for northbound yachts and Duke Robert of Normandy is rumoured to have anchored his fleet here in 1030, prior to a planned crossing of the Channel. That cruise was called off, but his son, William, had more luck in 1066.

Portelet

WANT TO SEE SOME ROCKS? The route into Portelet, between Pleinmont Point and the Hanois lighthouse, looks horrible on the chart but some of those rocks could act as helpful signposts for anyone who gets lost.

There is a maze of established transits to guide boats around this corner of Guernsey. They are shown on Chart 807 but most of their leading marks are lumps of rock. A stranger using the transits for the first time will face the inevitable problem of deciding which lump is which. In particular, a transit that leads past Hayes Rock and Round Rock uses the outer rock west of Lihou Island in line with Nipple Rock (dries 8.5m) on 010°. These marks may be difficult to identify in hazy weather or when large areas of the reefs are uncovered.

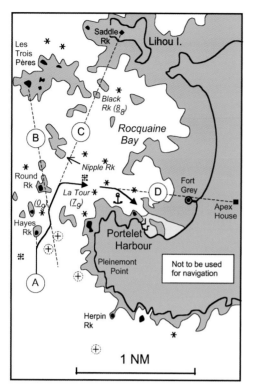

Fig 62 Approaches to Portelet Harbour, Guernsey.

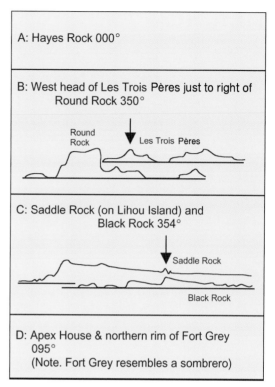

A: Hayes Rock 000°

B: West head of Les Trois Pères just to right of Round Rock 350°

Round Rock   Les Trois Pères

C: Saddle Rock (on Lihou Island) and Black Rock 354°

Saddle Rock

Black Rock

D: Apex House & northern rim of Fort Grey 095°
(Note. Fort Grey resembles a sombrero)

Fig 63 Bearing line and transits for the approach to Portelet Harbour (see Fig 62).

Fortunately, three prominent rocks lie close to the track. These are Hayes Rock (1m), Round Rock (7m) and La Tour (dries 7.9m). The last one covers at springs but if the trip to Portelet is made on a falling tide it should be exposed to view (MHWN is 6.7m and MHWS is 9.0m). We have made the passage as shown on the sketch plan, starting by approaching Hayes Rock on a bearing of 000° (Line A). This is the nearest of the offshore rocks and should be unmistakable. When within about 100m of Hayes Rock, one can diverge towards the north-east until on Line B, which leads to the east of a 0.9m drying rock. The exact track of the divergence is not critical, provided one does not progress far beyond Hayes Rock before reaching Line B. While on Line B, identify La Tour and the marks for Line C (see Figure 62). While on Line C, identify the marks for Line D. If, for any reason, Line C or Line D is difficult to identify, La Tour will serve as a turning mark. If visibility closes down to a mile or less, the transits will be obscured but a skipper who has found his way in to Portelet could probably find his way out again along the same track, by using the three key rocks as beacons.

For the final approach to Portelet Harbour, look for the lines of moored boats that lie in the fairway between the rocks. The harbour itself consists of low walls that cover at high tide but give some half-tide protection against swell: useful for landing from a tender but offering no shelter for yachts. It may be possible to anchor in the fairway at low water but a stay through high water would require more swinging room, which can be found a short distance to the west of the harbour.

HERM

This is a privately run but hospitable estate, like a smaller version of Tresco in the Isles of Scilly, and where facilities provided for campers and other holidaymakers are equally useful for yachts. Provisions are sold from a shop at the Mermaid tavern, close to the small harbour, and there is a freshwater tap nearby. Herm is another island with extensive reefs on one side, in this case on the north. The principal anchorages offer shelter from north-east and west.

Rosière Steps

BETWEEN HERM AND JETHOU, the tidal stream runs to the south-east for about 9 hours out of every 12. The current has scoured a gully between Mouette and Herm, and the Rosière Steps offer a low-tide landing place for the ferries. Some local moorings are laid immediately north of the steps but there

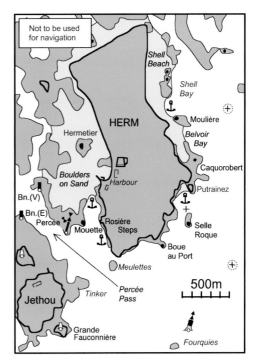

Fig 64 Herm.

The pool at Rosière Steps, Herm.

is usually room for about a dozen yachts to anchor north of these moorings. There is also a deeper anchorage, often used by larger vessels, to the south of the steps and close to the flank of Herm.

From the west, the Rosière Steps are approached via the Percée Pass, using traditional transits that are shown on the large-scale charts. At dead low water, before turning into the pool, take care to clear a shallow sandbank that lies south of Mouette. The entrance from the east is between the Tinker shoal and the Meulettes, which can both be avoided by steering to keep Hermetier in the middle of the gap between Mouette and Herm.

Beyond the northern end of the pool, the foreshore uncovers at low spring tides, roughly during the short period when the stream through the Percée Pass is flowing to the north-west. This means that on many days there is hardly any north-west flow through the pool. It is sheltered from north-east winds and is often surprisingly calm when the wind is in the north-west or west, possibly because waves are disrupted by the combination of rocks and strong currents. However, winds from between east and south-west send waves into the pool from the south. When the current compresses these waves to form mild overfalls, the anchorage becomes uncomfortable.

At low tide, the pool is a pleasant place for swimming, paddling or messing about in dinghies, and it should be possible to inspect the natural gatepost on Roche Percée (Gate Rock). According to local tradition, this stone with a hole was once a real gatepost, before the sea level rose. North of the pool, the foreshore sand is largely covered with stones and small boulders, so it is not easy to select a drying berth, although there are some small cleared areas near to the harbour where visiting yachts can moor to buoys or ground chains.

Putrainez

THIS IS A SMALL ANCHORAGE but we found it very agreeable when we approached Herm in a north-west wind and fairly thick mist. After a chilly passage, the small cove inshore of Putrainez provided welcome shelter and the mist was 'lifting off' as it blew over the island, so that we lay in a private patch of sunshine. The current UKHO charts show the foreshore as rock but there was a wide area of sand at the time of our visit.

Shell Bay

BELVOIR BAY IS OFTEN USED AS AN ANCHORAGE but the deep water is well offshore, out in the strong tidal streams. Not long ago, a yacht was lost when she anchored too close to the beach. She touched the ground under calm conditions but was then wrecked by swell, which increased suddenly. Immediately to the north of Belvoir, the bight at the southern end of Shell Beach offers better protection and relatively deep water closer to the shore.

Shell Bay is usually approached from the south, using Selle Roque and Caquorobert for general guidance. The rock spur between Putrainez and Caquorobert dries by 8.5m, so it will be uncovered at most times. When it is not, it can be avoided by using a clearance transit: Grande Fauconnière white beacon open to the left of Herm. To enter the anchorage, pass fairly close to the north of Moulière on a track of 270°, look for the drying

Shell Beach, Herm.

ledge that lies about 200m to the north of Moulière, and then select a position between the two. Anchors bury easily in the loose sand, although their dragging resistance may be lower than in dense materials. The depth is about 0.5m at LAT, so deep-draught yachts have to lie further offshore at spring tides. The anchorage is sheltered from between south-west and north-west, with reasonably good protection from westerly swell, although some swell comes around the north of the island at high tide.

Shoal-draught yachts and multihulls sometimes dry out in the middle of the beach. It is probably advisable to moor so as to take the ground at about half-tide and lift off again before the northern reefs are fully covered.

There is a small café on the edge of the dunes but the main attraction is the beach itself, largely consisting of shells and shell fragments. The best specimens were probably removed long ago but there are plenty of elongated tusk shells, and children enjoy being let loose with a collecting bucket.

SARK

Sark has no all-weather harbour but it does possess anchorages to suit all wind directions. The cliff scenery is spectacular and the island resembles a pie with a smooth top but a very crusty rim. Provisions are available from shops in the middle of the island and there is a freshwater tap at Creux Harbour.

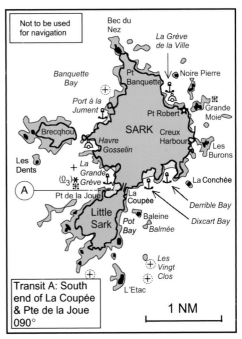

Fig 65 Sark.

North-West Quadrant

THE MIDDLE OF BANQUETTE BAY IS FREE OF DRYING ROCKS, although there are some patches that have less than 2m depth at LAT and drying outliers within about 200m of the shore. The best shelter for winds from east or south is in Port à la Jument. The entrance is straightforward but look out for small buoys, which may mark nets laid across the bottom. This sector of Sark is not notably popular with yachts, possibly because it is open to westerly swell, but probably also because a wind from the south or south-east is often expected to veer, strengthen and bring rain.

North-East Quadrant

LA GRÈVE DE LA VILLE OFFERS SHELTER FROM THE SOUTH-WEST and some visitors' mooring buoys have been installed. However, winds from the south-west are often accompanied by sizeable waves and this anchorage is notorious for 'rolly' conditions. If the bay is crowded, latecomers anchoring in a depth of about 8m will require a generous amount of swinging room. The northern entrance is a clean gap between Point Banquette and Noire Pierre but the narrow southern doorway, between Point Robert and Grande Moie, is partly obstructed by drying ledges. Navigation between Point Robert and Creux Harbour demands close attention to a large-scale chart.

South-East Quadrant

THIS SECTOR IS LIKELY TO BE FREQUENTED BY YACHTS during spells of northerly winds, which are usually associated with fine weather – ideal for appreciating those cliffs and beaches. Entry from the east is via the wide, clean gap between La Conchée and Baleine. The approach from the south is partly obstructed by Les Vingt Clos, which dry by 1.9m, but in limited visibility we have previously used L'Etac as a beacon, steering close to its east side and then inshore via Pot Bay.

The usual anchorages and landing places are in Dixcart and Derrible Bays, of which Dixcart has the easier path up the cliffs. At neap tides there is sufficient depth to lie afloat well inside both bays, when they offer some protection from the north-east. Westerly swell can work its way around the south of Sark and it often seems to be more noticeable in Dixcart, for some reason, possibly a consequence of the waves being refracted by a shallow bank to the north of Baleine.

South-West Quadrant

THE SECTOR INCLUDES LA GRANDE GRÈVE, which in easterly winds is arguably the best anchorage in the Channel Islands. Several rocks lie in the middle of the entrance but they dry by only 0.3m or less, so are well covered at half-tide. For entering the bay near to low water springs, one can use a southern track via Transit A (see Figure 65). An

La Grande Grève, Sark.

alternative approach is by passing close to Les Dents, which are steep-to and always above water, and thence into the northern half of the bay.

Most yachts anchor off the beach below the narrow isthmus of La Coupée but foreshore rocks intrude from either side. Slightly to the north of the beach, there is deep water close to the cliffs and the bottom is clean sand. The usual landing place is on the beach below La Coupée, from which a long flight of steps leads to the top of the pie crust.

Westerly swell may hamper beach landings by dinghy but is generally least noticeable around low tide, probably because the offshore tidal streams run towards the south-west from roughly half-tide falling until half-tide rising. Immediately to the north, Havre Gosselin has landing steps which can often be used when swell would make the beach impractical, but this inlet is now partly occupied by visitors' buoys.

JERSEY

The largest of the Channel Islands has several coastal towns with support facilities for itinerant yachts. St Helier is dominant but provisions may also be obtained at Gorey, St Aubin and St Brelade, and at some villages along the northern coast. There are anchorages on every side of the island, although we shall have to skip past the western beach of St Ouen Bay because whenever I have been there, it has been more suitable for surfing.

The North Coast

UNDER THE HIGH WALL OF JERSEY'S NORTHERN CLIFFS, the coastal indentations at Grève de Lecq, Bonne Nuit Bay, Bouley Bay and Rozel are traditional venues for daytime excursions in fine weather. There are several drying shoals within half a mile of the cliffs, including some in the approach to each of these anchorages, but pilotage is not particularly difficult. A decision to use any of these places for an overnight stop is more likely to be governed by the sea state.

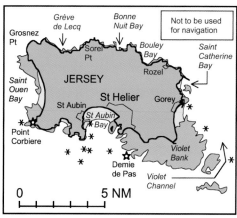

Fig 66 Jersey.

I can only claim personal knowledge of Bouley Bay and Rozel but our experience at the former was salutary. We had approached from the east with the ebb tide, anchored under fairly calm conditions and rowed ashore to the beach. After strolling up the hill to buy some provisions in the nearest village shop, we returned for a lazy lunch and the anchorage was still placid. However, about an hour after the tidal stream reversed, to flow along the coast from the west, waves in the bay increased dramatically and our boat started to pitch and roll, even dipping its stemhead under some of the crests. It was clear that swell had earlier been refracted away from the north coast by the ebb stream, but had returned with the flood.

Rozel has marginally better protection from the west but the best anchoring area, outside the harbour, is partly occupied by moored boats and keep boxes. Under calm conditions, it is a very pleasant spot but, unless swell is minimal, our next anchorage may be more comfortable for an extended stay.

St Catherine Bay

THE HARBOUR AT GOREY, overlooked by Mont Orgueil Castle, is picturesque and popular but feels quite exposed when a south-west wind whistles across the corner of the island. The visitors' moorings are on drying sand and the deeper anchorage, east of the breakwater, feels even more exposed. Immediately north of Gorey, St Catherine Bay has deep water closer to the shore and is one of the best anchorages in the Channel Islands for winds from south-west or west.

The bay's shelter was improved in the nineteenth century by the construction of its long northern breakwater. The project was intended to produce a naval harbour to supplement Portland and Braye, but it appears to have been completely misconceived and was finally abandoned. The incomplete stump of a second breakwater extends from the southern shore, close to the red and white Archirondel Tower, and nobody ever got around to removing the rocks in the middle of the bay. As it is, the completed breakwater does provide enhanced protection from the north-west, although waves from the north can turn into the bay by diffracting around the end of the wall.

The usual boat entrance is at the northern end, fairly close to the breakwater but avoiding the outlier of Pillon Rock and some rocks near to the breakwater wall. Moorings are laid south of the breakwater and inshore of the St Catherine Bank, all of them to seaward of the drying line so that the boats cannot pound on the sand when the wind is from the east. (Incidentally, many of these moorings use stainless steel chain, which tells a tale of mayhem in strong easterlies, with a fetch of about 15 miles from the coast of France.) For an approach from the south, we have used the line shown on Figure 67, passing between the Archirondel breakwater and a rock ledge that dries by 3.7m.

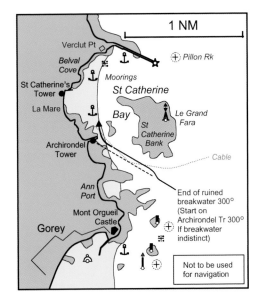

Fig 67 St Catherine Bay.

There are some clear spaces between the moorings and close to the root of the northern breakwater but on most tides it is also possible to anchor inshore of the moorings. In fact St Catherine provides a perfect instance of an anchorage that is widened by neap tides. In the central cove at La Mare, close to the inshore lifeboat station, the upper beach is steep shingle and pebbles but the lower beach, of gently shelving firm sand, remains well covered at neaps. MLWN is 4.3m and there is often sufficient depth to lie afloat close inshore, off Belval Cove or La Mare, with the luxury of unrestricted swinging room.

There are slipways at La Mare and inside the northern breakwater. At Verclut Point the St Catherine Sailing Club and the Jersey Canoe Club share a building that was originally used as a hospital and carpenter's shop during construction of the breakwater. There is also a café but the public water taps are marked as unfit for drinking. The nearest source of provisions and fresh water is Gorey, where the row of shops below the castle sells refreshments, meals and trinkets but the village proper is behind the coast road, half a mile to the south-west.

Belcroute Bay

WHEN ST HELIER IS TOO HOT AND BUSTLING, the harbour of St Aubin is a quiet alternative with fairly good facilities for yachts, but it dries by nearly 7m. MHWN is only 8.1m and on two occasions, when attempting to enter the harbour at very neap tides, we have found insufficient depth even to reach the visitors' berth. Immediately to the south, Belcroute Bay is protected from the west. It all dries at chart datum but the firm sand generally slopes from north to south. Close to the southern shore it is between 1m and 2m above datum, giving most yachts sufficient depth to lie afloat at neaps (MLWN is 4.1m). There are several moorings in this area but we have previously found space to anchor close to the south-west corner, where the tree-covered shore provides excellent

Belcroute Bay, Jersey – anchored in the sheltered south-west corner of the bay at low water neaps.

shelter. From the slipway here, a walk into St Aubin entails a short uphill detour because the western side of the bay is overlooked by private land. It is also possible to walk along the beach, although this route is cut off at high water. For tides other than neaps, there are greater depths further offshore close to Point de But, although this outer anchorage experiences more swell, particularly at high water, and is partly occupied by moorings, some of which appear to need maintenance.

Further north there are some isolated rocks within the bay. On Figure 68, I have shown one with a probable drying height of 5.4m (my estimate) because the charts do not give it a value. Eyeball pilotage may be difficult because the bay often fills with seawater that is slightly silty and opaque. However, the causeway inshore of St Aubin Fort is nearly 6m above datum. When there is enough depth to cross the causeway and its adjacent sand bar, or to enter the harbour, the obstacles in the middle of the bay should be adequately covered. Note that in the ridge of rocks to the south of the causeway, the highest rocks are *between* the two cardinal beacons, so that one should pass fairly close *outside* these beacons, where the foreshore level is roughly the same as the sand bar by the causeway. Current charts show the eastern beacon too far south and in 2003 it had lost its topmark, so some confusion is excusable.

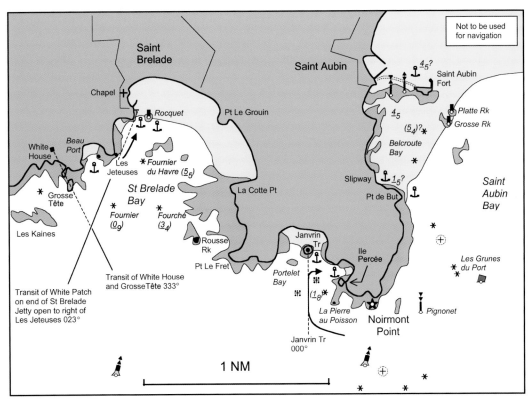

Fig 68 St Brelade, Portelet and Belcroute Bays.

I would not choose to take the ground within the bay because the high-speed catamaran ferries create a very heavy wash that breaks all along the shore. The best drying anchorage is close to the north of the fort, where a few local boats are moored behind the fort's eastern breakwater.

Portelet Bay

THIS IS A POPULAR PICNIC SPOT, where yachts often anchor alongside the central island. The inlet on the eastern side of the bay, north of the outcrop known as Ile Percée, is quite small but potentially useful because it is the only anchorage on Jersey's southern coast that provides good shelter in brisk east winds.

At high tide it may be possible to approach the anchorage by simply steering around La Pierre au Poisson, a prominent foreshore rock south-west of Ile Percée. The charts show this rock as covering at MHWS (11.1m) but the OS map shows it as 'dry' at MHW (9.6m), so its head is probably about 10m above chart datum. At lower heights of tide it is necessary to avoid a rock drying by 1.8m and two other lumps that are awash at LAT. We have entered by following a bearing of 000° on the Janvrin Tower, before turning into the anchorage.

St Brelade Bay

BEING OPEN TO THE SOUTH-WEST, this bay is likely to be uncomfortable at high water when there is any swell. In fine weather, given a flat sea or low tide, it is extremely pleasant, with a choice of beaches. Provisions are available from St Brelade, where there are restaurants and small shops near to the shore and the shopping centre of Red Houses is half a mile inland.

Several patches of drying rocks obstruct the middle of the bay. The usual anchorages are on the western side and Figure 68 shows entry lines that we have used. It can be seen that the line of bearing on Grosse Tête need not be exact. Les Jeteuses are jagged rock stacks at the eastern headland of Beau Port and here there is a clear width of about 200m between the shore and the nearest detached shoals.

The anchorage in Beau Port, alongside the elegant Pinnacle Rock, is a good mid-day suntrap. Some boulders lie on the beach, close to the drying line, so care is required when anchoring close inshore.

Towards the north-west corner of the bay, the usual anchorage is south of the stone jetty and the Rocquet beacon, although at neap tides it is possible to lie afloat slightly further north. Right in the corner, the medieval Fishermen's Chapel of St Brelade overlooks an ancient, half-tide mole where boats still moor to tree trunks set in the masonry, although the boats are now plastic. Cars and trailer-launched powerboats park on the beach but the chapel remains serene. Inside the adjacent (slightly younger) church, the walls are raw red granite that seems to glow in the restrained lighting. They were once plastered over but removal of the plaster has revealed several medieval limpets, indicating that the masons did not go far for their supplies of stone.

Portelet Bay, Jersey – the anchorage in the eastern corner, north of Ile Percée.

Beau Port, on the western side of Jersey's St Brelade Bay.

THE BIG REEFS

Many yachtsmen regard the detached reefs of Les Écrehou and the Plateau des Minquiers with a certain amount of awe. They are potentially hazardous, each a mass of imprecisely charted rocks swept by powerful tidal streams and largely invisible at high water. Never-theless, boats from Jersey and France frequent both places, Les Écrehou becoming positively crowded on fine summer weekends.

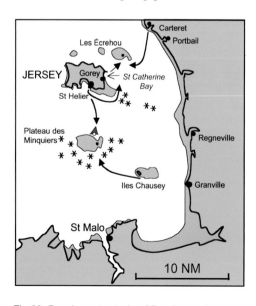

Fig 69 Popular routes to Les Minquiers and Les Écrehou.

To enjoy these huge rockeries, the locals work the tides. On each reef at high water, only a few spikes and lumps show above the sea, the visible heads are surrounded by broken water and strong currents boil over the many other menaces that lie just below the surface. Some of the larger lumps support tiny huts that were constructed by fishermen and quarrymen, but landing from a boat is difficult or dangerous in the slightest swell. A few hours later the prospect is transformed, as the ebb uncovers Atlantis. The exposed rocks provide protection, so that boats can approach slowly on flat water with the stream slackening, and skippers can take their time to identify the marks.

It is normal to leave Jersey or the mainland at about high water, in order to spend the low water period at a reef. From St Helier, a yacht can carry the late flood eastward, around the Violet Bank, and then ride the ebb north to Les Écrehou, the procedure being approximately reversed for the return. A passage from Gorey or St Catherine is much shorter and avoids the need to circumvent the Violet Bank. From the Iles Chausey, French boats make a comparable down-tide trip to the Minkies. Passages from Carteret to Les Écrehou or from Jersey to the Minkies will entail ferry-gliding across the currents but it should not be necessary to actually fight against a foul stream.

Les Écrehou

FIGURE 70 SHOWS THE USUAL ENTRY TRANSITS FROM THE SOUTH. They intersect close to a drying rock and I am inclined to cut the corner slightly, as shown. From Carteret the deep-water route is around the southern end of the Écrevière Bank but we have also crossed it at a height of tide of 4.2m. We had sufficient depth to clear the bank, which charts show as drying by 2.3m, while Grande Noire and Petite Noire were exposed to view and could therefore be adopted as pilotage marks. Our boat only draws 1.0m and good through-water visibility allowed us to distinguish the higher parts of the bank. This route is used by some French yachts but should not be contemplated if there is any swell. Please also note that the bank is formed as a series of ridges and valleys, so depths may vary abruptly within a few metres. Other French boats use a track that passes through the reef close to the north of L'Écrevière Rock, but we have not had an opportunity to inspect that area at low spring tides.

There are stone huts on Marmotière and two smaller islets to its north, leased to Jersey residents and used for holiday accommodation. The deep anchorage is south of Marmotière, but local moorings occupy part of the space and visiting boats have in the past become tangled with these buoys when they anchored too close. At half-ebb and later, the north-flowing stream is relatively gentle to the south of Marmotière, but rushes swiftly past its eastern side. Some yachts head for a pool within the reef, which is situated SSW of Marmotière and retains water to a depth of about 1m. It is normally approached at about half-tide, steering up a narrow gully between the rocks Le Fou and Pommère, both of which dry by about 5m (my estimate). At this stage of the tide the gully and the rocks should be visible under the water and a current flows out of the pool to join the main ebb that is

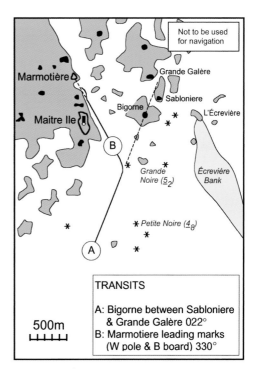

Fig 70 Les Écrehou – approaches from the south.

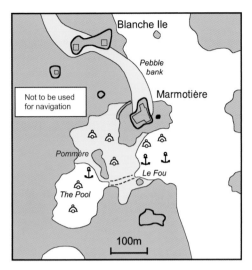

Fig 71 Marmotière moorings and anchorages.

spilling around Marmotière. Entry to the pool can be made slowly, against the stream.

Moorings are laid in the pool and on most of the patches of drying sand, between the rocks. Their gear is generally designed to control swinging room, so that the boats stay within the small areas of sand. A common arrangement is a chain or wire cable spanning between rocks, with a riser secured to the middle of the span. It may be possible to borrow a mooring but anchors should only be set in positions that are clear of the permanent ground tackle.

At low tide in fine weather, visiting crews and the temporary inhabitants of the huts spread out across the reef to explore and to collect shellfish. The miniscule buildings are very close to high water level but the wide reef disrupts big waves, so that the sea cannot quite destroy Jersey's northern colony. There is a very small garden plot between the huts, with a soil area of about one square metre. It has occasionally been washed away.

At about low water the stream slackens, before reversing to flow south. To the south of Marmotière, a powerful eddy is set up within the anchorage until the bank beyond the pool becomes covered, then part of the stream starts to flow through the pool. By high water the stream has reversed again and is flowing north. At springs this current is strong on each side of Marmotière, and the pebble ridge to Blanche Ile becomes covered. As the level drops and the pebble banks to the north uncover, the stream from the pool flows eastward again, around the south of Marmotière, and continues to do so until low water.

Les Écrehou, looking SSW from Marmotière towards the eastern corner of Jersey. Le Fou is the small rock on the left-hand side of the photograph and Pommère is right of centre, with the Pool beyond it.

Les Minquiers

THE MINKIES ARE LESS POPULAR THAN LES ÉCREHOU. The huts are all on Maitresse Ile and in the past have been occupied less frequently. A few have recently been modernised, displaying evidence of cavity insulation and other luxuries.

The pilotage for the usual entry tracks is not difficult but it is important to plan in terms of height of tide. The sketch plan shows an approximate outline of the main hazards in the area near to Maitresse Ile. The beacons are drawn on the basis on my own compass survey, as UKHO Chart 3656 is on a small scale and has for many years shown some of these beacons in the wrong positions. Nevertheless, that chart is essential for other details and for the approach from north or south. A new edition should be published at about the same time as this book.

When coming from Jersey, the approach is commenced from the Demie de Vascelin buoy (to the north of the sketch plan), steering towards Jetée des Fontaines de Bas with that beacon in transit with the northern flagstaff on Maitresse Ile. When (say) 200m short of Jetée des Fontaines de Bas, turn to starboard and track towards the Grune Tar beacon until on the transit of the Rocher du Sud Bas beacons. This transit used to run across relatively deep water, but sandbanks have encroached from the west and, in late 2003, the sand to the north-west of Grune Tar on this transit dried by approximately 4m. If the height of tide is too low for crossing this bank, it may be possible to find a deeper route around its eastern edge but that is fairly close to some of the rocks.

The initial approach from the south simply leads along the Rocher du Sud Bas transit from the other direction. The beacons are clearly painted but binoculars may be useful, as it is necessary to pick up this line more than a mile to the south. The detached rock about 300m to the south of the beacons dries by approximately 3.8m (my estimate). The diversion shown on the sketch plan is as drawn on the UKHO chart but has no marks. When we tried to follow this zigzag as closely as possible, starting the first turn when Petit Rocher du Sud Bas was abeam, we found the shallowest point was roughly 1m below chart

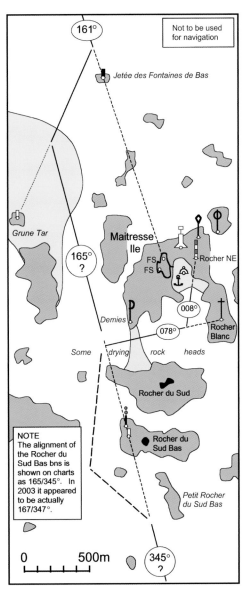

Fig 72 Plateau des Minquiers – approaches to Maitresse Ile.

Within the figure:
161°
Not to be used for navigation
Jetée des Fontaines de Bas
Grune Tar
165° ?
Maitresse Ile
FS
FS
Rocher NE
Demies
008°
078°
Rocher Blanc
Some drying rock heads
Rocher du Sud
Rocher du Sud Bas
NOTE
The alignment of the Rocher du Sud Bas bns is shown on charts as 165/345°. In 2003 it appeared to be actually 167/347°.
Petit Rocher du Sud Bas
0   500m
345° ?

datum. The predicted height of tide was 3.6m and we did not see the submerged western extremity of Rocher du Sud or the detached rock close to its west, but I am prepared to believe that they both exist, probably close to chart datum.

The north and south approaches meet to the south-west of the Demies beacon. The next leg is directly towards the Rocher Blanc beacon (which is sometimes supplemented by a front mark, painted either white or fluorescent orange) and crosses a sandbank south of Demies. In 2003 the bank dried by 1.2m at this point, but was higher to the south.

The final line leads towards Rocher NE and it is necessary to diverge into the anchorage, on a patch of soft sand between Maitresse Ile and Rocher NE. There is a States of Jersey mooring buoy and the sand around it dries by approximately 1m. Most yachts would be able to lie afloat there at neaps (MLWN is 4.1m).

It can be seen that the northern approach requires sufficient height of tide to cross the sandbank north-west of Grune Tar. For the southern approach, the entry is actually easier

Les Minquiers – the anchorage area by Maitresse Ile, at low water neaps. *London Apprentice* is lying to the States of Jersey mooring buoy.

when the 3.8m drying rock is exposed to view, but there must be sufficient water to cross the bank south of Demies. A height of tide in excess of 6m (plus whatever safety margin you wish to add) would appear to give adequate cover over all these obstacles.

At low tide, the anchorage between Maitresse Ile and Rocher NE is well sheltered from the west and out of the stronger currents. The usual landing place is the long concrete slip, although there may be some wave action even at low tide. The rock ridge between Maitresse Ile and Rocher NE dries by approximately 5.5m. When it is covered, currents run through this gap, the anchorage loses most of its protection and landing is likely to be risky.

On Maitresse Ile, apart from the various huts, there is a helicopter landing pad, an old customs post and the famous WC that is the most southerly building in the British Isles.

15 Anchors

When anchors are subjected to comparative trials, the test procedures usually measure the maximum load that each anchor can resist when it is laid on a uniform bed of fairly soft material. It is implicitly assumed that the highest load indicates the best anchor. However, during many years of cruising, using anchors regularly, we have never experienced our anchor dragging under a high load when it was properly embedded. In practice, dragging is more likely to occur because the anchor has not embedded properly, or because it has been tripped out of the seabed by a change in the direction of load, or because it has been fouled. Some types of anchors appear to be more susceptible than others to these failings. Of course, in exposed anchorages, very high winds and pronounced wave action, a skipper will be rightly anxious about the ultimate holding power of an anchor. Under all other conditions, it may be more important that the anchor is tolerant of different seabeds and does not exhibit any notable bad habits.

Over the last few decades, a considerable number of anchor tests have been carried out – by official bodies, by anchor manufacturers and by yachting magazines. Certain consistent patterns have emerged, but most of the tests have been undertaken on sand and few have been done in weedy areas or on multi-layer materials, such as thin silt over clay. It would probably be difficult to ensure consistent test conditions on such seabeds but they are highly relevant to real cruising. In the absence of test results, data must be obtained by observing anchors in use. Whenever we have dragged, or have seen other boats dragging, I have attempted to deduce the most likely causes by correlating any available evidence such as anchor type, cable scope, changes in direction of load, seabed materials, etc. The following notes are based on documented tests and personal observations, supplemented by reports from other seafarers who have had experience of using particular anchors.

Anchor types

I categorise anchors in four groups, as below:

1 Narrow flukes (eg Fisherman anchor and grapnel).
2 Flat-bladed and articulated (eg Danforth and Britany).
3 Plough (eg CQR and derivative designs).
4 Single fluke, rigid (eg Bruce, Delta and Spade).

Seabed types

Seabed characteristics are infinitely variable but the following simplified descriptions can be related to typical anchor behaviour:

- *Hard* Rock and densely packed boulders.
- *Soft* Sand, shingle and mud.
- *Dense surface* Hard sand, shaley gravel or similar, possibly covering a softer substrate.

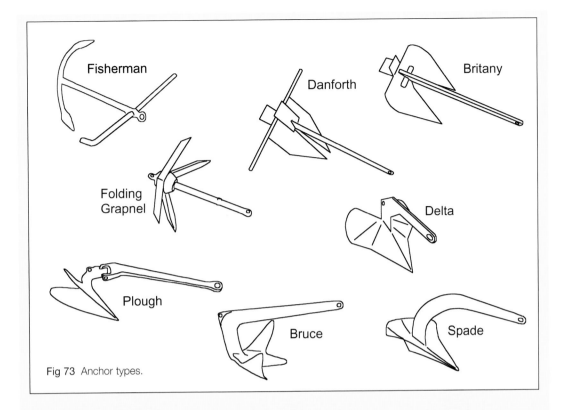

Fisherman

Danforth

Britany

Folding
Grapnel

Delta

Plough

Bruce

Spade

Fig 73 Anchor types.

- *Soft covering* Soft silt or loose weed, above a firmer substrate.
- *Growing weed* Weed with stems or fronds connected to the seabed, as opposed to a semi-rotten mass of loose weed.

Anchors in action

A perfect anchor should hold securely on any seabed materials and should also be designed so that it is not easily fouled, whether by its own cable or by weed and debris. When the direction of load is reversed, it should turn without breaking out of the seabed, so that it can be trusted to re-set on its own initiative when its owner is ashore or asleep. To date, nobody has created a perfect anchor.

Anchors with narrow flukes are effective on rock, because their points lodge in minor crevices and they can also penetrate a certain depth of weed. However, the small fluke area limits their holding power in soft materials and their upward projections are vulnerable to fouling by their own cables. 'Improved' designs usually have larger

flukes but the problem of fouling appears to be insurmountable. We use a large grapnel as one of our kedge anchors because it will take hold quickly on almost any seabed material, although it will drag steadily through soft sand and shingle (eg Shell Bay and La Grande Grève).

Flat-bladed anchors hold well when embedded in soft materials, although if the surface is very dense they may lie flat without digging their points in. They are vulnerable to fouling by anything that gets between the shank and the twin blades, particularly if the anchor turns upside down and the hinge action is jammed, so that the blades cannot then swing downwards. This type of anchor may turn over if the direction of the applied load is reversed, as when the tide turns. From time to time we have been able to observe boats dragging their anchors in the vicinity of our own yacht, and have sometimes been able to assist them – and inspect their ground tackle. All except one have used a Danforth or similar anchor.

The widely spread blades of the Britany anchor

are intended to resist fouling. It has no transverse stock or stabilising bar and is prone to turning over if it is dragged through the seabed. If one blade starts to penetrate more than the other, it continues to do so, rotating the anchor until it is inverted. The Britany type is popular in France, where many coastal anchorages have beds of sand with some weed. If it is rarely subjected to loads that are sufficient to drag it through the seabed, it is possible that its users rarely experience the problem of rotation. Some comparable designs, such as the FOB THP, do incorporate a stabilising bar.

Most plough anchors hold well in soft materials. However, when a plough anchor is first lowered on to the seabed, the fluke rests on its side; it has to 'scoop' itself into the bottom before it will start to rotate and incline the point downwards. This makes it reluctant to engage with rock or to pierce dense surfaces and it may also slide through a very soft covering material, without penetrating any further. We have experienced these problems on very hard sand (eg Utah Beach), shaley gravel (the southern part of Barn Pool), soft silt over clay (eg Newtown River), and loose weed over sand (in various deep pools). Because the fluke often drags for some distance before becoming properly buried, it is quite likely to become fouled unless it is in an area free of weed. This risk recurs when the direction of load is reversed, as the anchor is liable to break out and again drag for a short distance before re-setting. Once, when using a CQR anchor at Dartmouth, we dragged for about 100m after the tide changed, ending up with another yacht's bowsprit nudging our backstay. On growing weed, the fluke may slide over the top of the vegetation without reaching the seabed. Nevertheless, this type of anchor resists fouling by its own cable because, even if the shank is not buried, it usually hinges to lie flat on the seabed.

When a plough anchor does become fouled, it is likely to drag freely. Of the various yachts that have dragged towards or past our own, the only one that was not using a Danforth type anchor was

using a CQR. It had (unbeknown to its owner), hooked on to an old hawser that was partly embedded in mud, on the Jaudy estuary. When a gust of wind increased the load on the anchor and 'unstuck' the hawser from the bottom, it remained looped around the fluke, which would not re-bury, and the yacht then hit us amidships!

The first successful single-fluke rigid anchor was the Bruce, initially developed for oilfield work. It was designed to bury quickly and hold on a short scope, which it does admirably in most soft materials. With its multiple points, it partly resembles a grapnel and has been used successfully on some hard bottoms. Growing weed can prevent it burying, however, because the stems or fronds lie between the separate points of the fluke. When broken out of a muddy bottom, it has been known to retain a tough ball of the seabed between its points, which may prevent it from re-burying.

The Delta anchor buries quickly in soft materials, sometimes slicing deep below the surface before developing its full resistance. Even if it initially lies on its side, its point is normally inclined downwards and makes immediate contact with the seabed, so that it buries point-first and can grip some rocky surfaces. Its single point is also capable of piercing a limited thickness of weed and we have known a Delta partly penetrate a thick mass of loose weed above firm sand. The soft covering material discouraged the fluke from burying but the point of the anchor lodged in the sand until the engine was put hard astern. It then dragged slowly but did not lose its hold completely. When the Delta is buried it resists becoming fouled under a reversal of load, because it will usually turn while remaining buried. However, if it is not buried properly, its own cable may catch either on the shank or the rear of the fluke. We have experienced this problem on a dense surface, after anchoring casually and without ensuring that the anchor was pulled into the seabed.

The Spade anchor appears to share the Delta's capacity for taking hold quickly and on mixed materials, also its ability to turn without breaking out. In tests on sand, it has consistently outperformed other types and its manufacturers attribute this success to the concave face of its fluke. However, in tests on a muddy bottom, that fluke retained a large lump of mud and would not re-bury after breaking out. This tendency of a concave fluke to retain mud is reminiscent of the Bruce. The rear of the fluke is formed as a smooth curve, and this anchor seems to be generally resistant to fouling by its own cable.

The Delta and the Spade appear to be 'near-perfect' anchors, each having one notable weakness; the Spade's fluke can be fouled by mud and the Delta can be fouled by its own cable. We have been using a Delta for the last few seasons and it has been very effective on most types of seabed. If it were redesigned with a tidier junction between shank and fluke, so that it was less likely to catch its own chain, it would be even better. As it is, we take care to pull it properly into the bottom, in order to control that risk.

Several of the anchors described above have been copied or imitated, and there are other anchors that combine the features of more than one type. In my view, complicated flanges and other projections are undesirable because they increase the risk of fouling. Some types of single-fluke anchor have the shank joining the fluke near to its point. This may enhance the strength of the anchor but is likely to limit its ability to penetrate weed.

Multiple anchors

We hardly ever lie to more than one anchor. Two anchors may reduce swinging room, but will cause problems in a crowded anchorage if adjacent yachts are lying to single anchors. The second anchor is more useful in a narrow cove or river channel where there are no nearby boats. If there is a significant risk of dragging, a second anchor may save the day but could also increase the chance of a tangle. It would certainly cause complications if we had to get under way in a hurry, during the hours of darkness.

The anchor chum

This device, sometimes known as an angel, is a weight that is slid down the anchor cable. It has been suggested that the added weight flattens the lower part of the cable's catenary curve, so that there is less chance of an upward force being exerted on the anchor, although some theoretical studies have thrown doubt on this explanation.

We have found that the most effective use of a chum is to prevent our boat snatching at its anchor when anchored in shallow water, where most of the chain lies on the bottom and a small downwind movement of the boat, yawing or surging in a gust, is sufficient to bring the cable almost taut. If the chum is suspended just above the seabed, the cable must lift the weight close to the surface as its tension increases. This extends the surge movement by two or three seconds and reduces the snatch loads. An alternative technique is to join a length of thin nylon warp to the chain and then veer more chain, so that the nylon can stretch to accommodate the variations in load. However, this increases the swinging circle, whereas the chum reduces it slightly and also discourages yawing.

16 North Brittany

This area is so convoluted, with deep estuaries leading inland and reefs fringing much of the coast, that it would almost justify a book in itself. Because many of the possible anchorages are immediately adjacent to harbours or within rivers, and are well described by existing publications, this chapter concentrates on the more ragged parts of the coastal fringe, where local boats flit between the tombstones but first-time visitors from across the Channel may feel slightly intimidated.

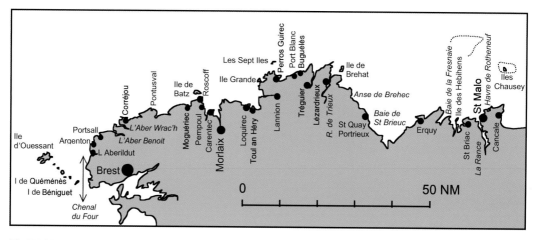

Fig 74 North Brittany.

ILES CHAUSEY TO ILE DE BRÉHAT

In this area, many of the drying inlets are partly obstructed by shellfish beds. Sheltered zones of deeper water are generally close to the harbours and largely occupied by moorings, although it may be possible to anchor to seaward of the moorings while retaining some of the shelter (eg north of Cancale, in westerly winds). The sandy estuaries at Havre de Rotheneuf and St Briac are well protected and have room for anchoring but dry completely at low spring tides.

There is a popular anchorage in a small bay on the eastern side of Ile des Hebihens, where the island is private but visitors may land on the beach. The best spot dries by about 1m, but MLWN is 4.1m so yachts are often able to tuck close inshore while remaining afloat at low water, with the island providing some protection from the north-west.

Shellfish beds cover the middle of the Baie de Fresnaie but a deepwater anchorage in the northern corner is protected from the north-west. Along this coast, there are many minor bays where the mainland provides general protection from the south but the roadstead off Erquy is almost unique in offering good shelter from the east. The ideal anchoring position would be close under the headland, west of the harbour breakwater, but look out for floating keep boxes.

On the western side of the Baie de St Brieuc, the general alignment of the coastline gives shelter from the west. The smaller bays, such as the Anse de Brehec, enhance that shelter but some westerly swell can find its way in from the north. Between St Malo and the Ile de Bréhat (see below), the only harbour offering complete protection and all-tide access is the marina at St Quay Portrieux.

For inland cruising, the estuary of the Rance has a number of attractive anchorages, although it is necessary to become accustomed to the eccentric tidal flows, dictated by the demands of the hydroelectric barrage. Shoal-draught yachts also have the option of taking a short cut to the Bay of Biscay via the canal network, but that would by-pass the really interesting bits of Brittany's northern coast.

The Back Lanes of Bréhat

STRADDLING THE ENTRANCES TO THE TRIEUX ESTUARY, the Ile de Bréhat is a famously picturesque jumble of orange rocks, fairytale villas, pine trees and flowers. (See Figure 75, page 146.) This is a favourite destination for many British cruisers and provisions can be purchased at the central hamlet of Le Bourg – not cheap, but probably quicker than going several miles up-river to Lézardrieux.

The island's narrow lanes are free of cars, although they fill with pedestrians when *vedettes* bring the daily contingent of tourists from the mainland. Similarly, in holiday periods, the principal anchorages become congested with yachts. However, it is possible to escape from the maritime crowds by exploring Bréhat's other lanes: navigable channels that lead between the small islands and big rocks of the neighbouring reefs.

To the south of the island, there are three traditional anchorages. Port Clos dries at low tide and is very busy during the daytime with *vedettes* coming and going. A little way to the east, there is a deep-water anchorage off Guerzido beach, outside a line of buoys that mark the bathing area. This is partly clear of the tide and has good holding on sand but is only sheltered from the north. The third anchorage is in the mouth of La Chambre, an inlet between Bréhat and Ile Logodec. Pole beacons (not shown on Figure 75) mark the rocks at the entrance but the inlet is largely filled with moorings and room to anchor is limited. Bréhat's most convenient freshwater tap is at the head of a slipway on the western side of La Chambre.

East of Ile Logodec is another, less well known anchorage where a gully leads into the reef. This anchorage is protected from the west. At neap tides yachts can lie afloat inside the gully, where it widens in several places. To seaward of the island, the above-water head of Men Bras Logodec helps to mark the edge of the reef.

To explore further, we need to take account of the rise and fall of tide. Most of the navigable back lanes are dry at low water, when their beds are paved with a mix of sand, stones and boulders, with occasional ridges of rock. There are also some deep pools but to reach them the most direct routes lead up and over the drying bits. A detailed chart is essential, preferably SHOM 7127, on a scale of 1:20,000, or UKHO 3673. The charts show very few bed levels in the drying channels, however, so a stranger must proceed carefully. The local tide levels are MHWS 10.3, MHWN 7.9, MLWN 3.6, MLWS 1.2.

Immediately north of La Chambre, there is a 'no anchoring' area where cables cross the channel. Slightly further on, just north of Ile Logodec, an area of firm and almost level sand forms an excellent drying anchorage (see photo on back cover). The bed is approximately 3.0m above chart datum but French yachts simply don their beaching legs. This anchorage has good protection from north, west and south, although it is partly open to the east at high tide, when the reef largely covers. For a first visit, it is advisable to bring up fairly close to the northern point of Ile Logodec and then inspect the bed at low water. Further north, much of the sand is in patches between loose stones and boulders, so alternative anchoring positions must be chosen with care. This spot can also be reached via the gully north of Ile Logodec, passing through a narrow 'gateway' between the rocks. There is quick access to Le Bourg by dinghy, via a gravel hard to the north-west of the anchorage. This used to be known as 'the English Strand', commemorating the landing of medieval raiders from the north.

The low water anchorage within Bréhat's western reefs, south of Ile Verte.

At high water, passenger *vedettes* cruise through the anchorage and continue via an S-bend around the north of Ile Lavrec. They stop running when the height of tide falls to about 6.5m. The chart does not show any drying level at the highest point of the pass and there are rocks projecting above the bed. We went through while observing the depths and the highest point that we recorded was approximately 4.5m above datum (my estimate, based on predicted height of tide). At high water there appears to be an adequate margin of safety but the line of the S-bend cannot be described in print and it would be helpful to walk the bed of the channel before a first passage.

Beyond Ile Lavrec, a wide, sandy channel leads north-east to Roc'h Louet, which is topped by a white beacon, and then out through the edge of the reef. Between Ile Lavrec and Roc'h Louet is a deep pool, not shown on the charts, with a depth of about 2m below datum and good protection from the west. A few moorings have been laid in the pool and there is also room to anchor. The rocks alongside the pool cover at high tide but one way to become familiar with this channel is to pass Ile Lavrec at high water, then anchor close to the north of the island, on soft sand, and wait as the tide falls. Before that anchoring

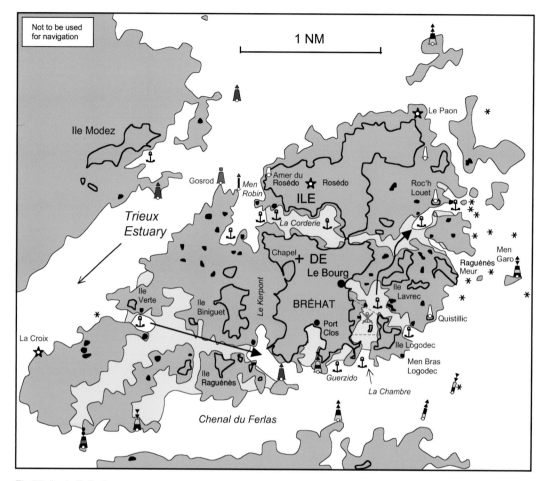

Fig 75 Ile de Bréhat.

position dries, it will be possible to make out the edges of the channel and the location of the pool. The ebb runs through the reef towards the north and boats in the pool generally lie to the north-east of their anchors until the stream slackens, shortly before low water.

This channel is partly obstructed by rocks south of Roc'h Louet but there is an even deeper anchorage about 200m further to the east, immediately alongside a prominent rock stack. Beyond this anchorage, rocks of all shapes and sizes obstruct the exit from the channel. We have passed through them with the aid of the SHOM chart, moving very slowly on flat water at low tide, and with a lookout on the bow, but this is not an easy option. An alternative exit (apart from returning around Ile Lavrec) is via a gully that runs to the south-east, past the northern side of the island of Raguénès Meur. This is more or less a straight line but there are half-tide ledges on each side and it would be advisable to inspect the route at low water. The easiest time for a stranger to use this channel would be shortly after low water, as soon as there is sufficient depth over the sandbanks in the gully. There are some isolated rocks to the east of the exit but they can be avoided by turning south, close to Raguénès Meur, and then following the edge of the reef past the white beacon of Quistillic.

These complicated reefs may horrify skippers who prefer wide channels and lots of man-made beacons. However, when one has overcome an initial sense of awe and learned to recognise the natural features, it is fascinating to explore the chaotic low-water landscape of contorted rocks, sandy beaches and deep, clear pools. Of course, it is possible to study the difficult bits from the tender while the yacht remains in a more conventional anchorage.

On the western side of Ile de Bréhat the principal anchorage is in La Corderie, which can be approached from the south via the drying channel of Le Kerpont. This used to be Bréhat's principal harbour, before tourist *vedettes* became important, and it may have been the main base for the local corsairs, who preyed on English merchant shipping in the eighteenth century. Both Le Kerpont and La Corderie are marked by pole beacons (mostly omitted from the sketch plan). La Corderie dries almost completely at low spring tides, although there is an overflow anchorage to its west, within the reef.

The Glénans sailing organisation has a base on Ile Verte and keeps small cruisers on moorings to the south of that island. From that position, a drying channel leads directly across the reef towards the southern end of Le Kerpont. At the western end of the channel, its entrance from the River Trieux lies between two rock heads that are exposed at MHWS and serve as gateposts, although there are lower outliers to their west. Immediately beyond the Glénans moorings, there is a sand bar (which dried by approximately 1.5m when we checked it) and then a deeper pool, with a depth of about 1m below datum. Here we were able to enjoy a relaxed low-water lunch well away from the August crowds, while a French picnic party adopted one of the nearby sandbanks as their own temporary desert island. The anchorage would probably have adequate protection at high tide if the wind was northerly and the swell slight.

From this anchorage, the channel leads in a straight line between Ile Raguénès and Ile Biniguet. For most of the way it is possible to use a low cliff, at the southern end of Ile de Bréhat, as a steering mark by keeping it just open of the islets to the south of the channel. However, the alignment of the various features changes as one progresses towards Le Kerpont, so the line should first be viewed at low tide, when the rubble banks and rocks close to the channel will be visible. The bed of the channel dries by nearly 4m (my estimate). A rock to the south of Ile Biniguet dries by about 6.5m and is fairly close to the channel.

On the western side of the Trieux entrance, the anchorage south of Ile Modez would be a convenient place to sit out the ebb before heading up-river, or to await the offshore ebb stream before setting off towards the west. In westerly winds it is placid at low tide but open to swell at high water.

ILE DE BRÉHAT TO LES SEPT ILES

Many of the yachts that visit this area head for Lézardrieux or Tréguier. In the lower reaches of the Trieux River, moorings now occupy the best anchoring positions and the shellfish beds have been extended in recent years. However, unobstructed deep water can be found in the Ledano reach, above the Lézardrieux suspension bridge, an area formerly worked by the sand dredgers and suitable for anchoring the largest of yachts. There is also a pleasant spot a mile further south, off the old river crossing point of Le Passage, and another at Roche Jagu, where boats often anchor on the sharp bend, overlooked by the magnificent Chateau Jago, but more swinging room can be found about 300m upstream.

The deeper pools may collect debris and we once found that our anchor chain had tied itself around a waterlogged tree trunk, so be prepared to disentangle unwanted anchor weights.

Tréguier's estuary, the River Jaudy, is narrower than that of the Trieux but it has less traffic and there are several deep anchorages in the main channel. East of Tréguier, the coast appears to be an unwelcoming mess of reefs, with the only straightforward inlet at Port Blanc (see below). Perros Guirec's marina gate closes for low water but at neap tides there is a fine anchorage outside the harbour, tucked inshore of the headland and beautifully sheltered from south and west. At Les Sept Iles, most of the archipelago is not only a nature reserve but also a prohibited area, although visitors are still permitted to anchor east of Ile aux Moines and to land on that island.

Buguélès and Port Blanc

PORT BLANC IS A POPULAR YACHT ANCHORAGE but there is another less well-known gap in the coastal reefs, immediately to its east, which is marked by a generous allocation of buoys and beacons. This is the Port of Buguélès, and it is linked to Port Blanc by a high water channel that leads inshore of a very decorative group of islands and pebble banks. For exploration, the best charts are SHOM 7125 and 7126, on a scale of 1:20,000.

In the approach to Buguélès, it is first necessary to avoid the Barr Laerez shoal, approximately one mile to the north. The entry is marked by the Basse Goulet Plat buoy, followed by a second starboard-hand buoy, and then there is a narrow gap between a port-hand buoy and a beacon on the small island of Enez Inic. Further inshore, everything dries at LAT but MLWN is 3.5m and MLWS is 1.2m, so it is often possible to lie afloat at low water, fairly close to the south of Enez Inic. This anchorage, on clean sand, is well sheltered from east, south and west, while the rock mass of Kastell Gwazou and its neighbours provides some protection from the north-west, particularly at neap tides. At the anchor symbol on the sketch plan, the bed is about 1.5m above chart datum. Further inshore, there is a group of drying moorings by a slipway.

Buguélès has a freshwater tap at the slip and a restaurant in the village but no shop selling provisions. West of the slip, a few yachts are moored in drying berths within a perfectly sheltered natural harbour, inshore of Ile Balanec and Ile Ozac'h. This inlet, overlooked by a disused tide mill, has a central channel between sloping beaches of sand, pebbles and stones, but could be used by visitors after a low-tide reconnaissance.

Port Blanc has deep water in its entrance channel, which leads between the reef outcrops from the NNW. It is open to north and north-west, so yachts often anchor in positions that gain enhanced protection from one side or the other, the most usual spot for neap tides being south of Ile St Gildas, where the sand is about 1m above datum. Freshwater taps are by the slipways at both ends of the village, a bar sells some provisions and there is also a baker with restricted opening hours.

Between Buguélès and Port Blanc the drying channels are completely protected by a barrier of islands, some of them joined by long, curving pebble banks. At high tide this becomes an inland sea, where dinghies and windsurfers can be sailed on flat water. Another partly sheltered area extends eastwards from Buguélès, inshore of Ile des Pins. Some of the islands have houses, generally used for holiday accommodation, but it is

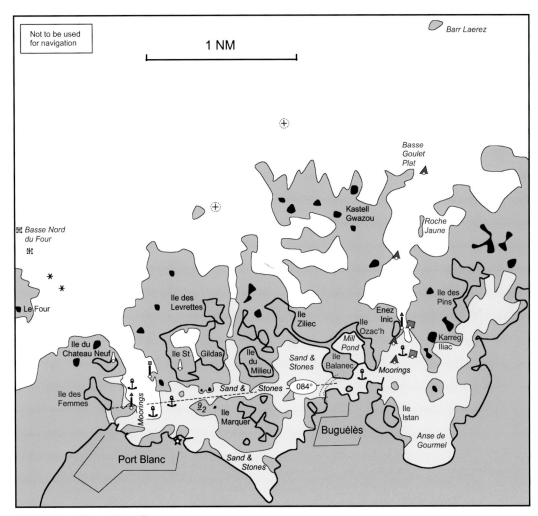

Fig 76 Buguélès and Port Blanc.

possible to walk on them fairly freely. The whole maze is reminiscent of Bréhat, but with fewer people. Some of the inner leads could be used as very exclusive drying anchorages but it would be advisable to make a prior inspection, at low tide, because there are patches of stones and small boulders lying on the sand.

A road from the mainland to Ile Balanec crosses a ford that dries by approximately 7.5m (my estimate). There used to be a low overhead cable but it appears to have been re-laid underground, so shoal-draught yachts can pass over the road at springs and dinghies can do so on most tides (MHWS is 9.5m and MHWN is 7.4m). The best approach, from Port Blanc, is a dead straight line as shown on the sketch chart. There are no suitable back marks to create transits but the line is obvious if viewed at low tide. To the south of Ile St Gildas, this line passes between two rock heads, one always above water and the other covered at MHWS. It crosses banks that dry by about 7.5m but they are no higher than the ford. For the return trip, the line is towards the head of the beach at the southern end of Ile des Femmes.

Buguélès – the natural harbour behind Ile Balanec and Ile Ozac'h. At high spring tides this waterway leads through to Port Blanc, inshore of the islands.

LES SEPT ILES TO ILE DE BATZ

West of Les Sept Iles, the reefs around Ile Grande (see below) provide opportunities for intricate explorations and then the wide bay between Ile Grande and Ile de Batz gives access to some more estuaries.

In the Lannion River, the traditional anchorage immediately inside the narrow mouth is now filled with moorings. Further upstream there is still room to anchor with adequate depths to lie afloat, particularly at neap tides, although it may be necessary to row back to the entrance in order to get ashore. This river is not at its best in stiff westerly winds, which funnel up the valley, but is lovely in fine weather.

A few miles to the south, at the entrance to the River Douron, the village of Locquirec has shops and even a bank. The usual anchorage, just inside the northern corner of the bay, is sheltered from the west. At neaps it is possible to lie afloat further south, near to the village, and there is also unlimited sand for drying berths. If the wind comes in from the north-west, twin-keeled yachts can retreat further up the Douron to the inner basin at the hamlet of Toul an Héry, where there is a crumbling barge quay but also a good drying anchorage on soft sand in the bed of the river. The substantial town of Plestin les Grèves is one mile inland.

Within the Morlaix estuary and the adjacent Penzé River there are anchorages to suit all wind directions except north. In the outer reaches of these estuaries most of the deep-water channels are a long way from the land, so that conditions feel distinctly draughty if the wind is fresh. At neap tides, it is easier to find cosy corners. On the northern side of Carentec, for instance, the deep-water anchorage is half a mile offshore, but at neaps we were able to lie afloat within 100m of the town while a strong south-westerly wind whistled overhead.

On the western side of the Penzé estuary, the harbour of Pempoul offers sheltered drying berths, with the facilities of St Pol de Léon just up the hill. Roscoff is the principal local harbour but it, too, dries completely. Forget the deepwater ferry port, because yachts are definitely not welcome there. If we wish to avoid the dust of Roscoff's quayside car parks, we may as well go across the Canal de Batz to the quieter harbour on Ile de Batz. The best drying anchorage is in the northern part of the harbour, on an area of sand. The shops are small but fresh water is available and we can go up the semaphore tower to admire the wild view to the west, while we wait for a favourable wind shift to take us around the corner of Brittany. Alternatively, if the waiting is prolonged, we may as well go back to have a look at Ile Grande.

Ile Grande

THIS LOW-LYING ISLAND IS JOINED TO THE MAINLAND by a causeway and surrounded by minor islets, rocks and sand-filled channels but there are at least two attractive deep-water anchorages. The coast is very exposed to westerly swell and therefore all the natural breakwaters are valuable. SHOM Charts 7124 and 7125 give a fairly good level of detail, although certain omissions and errors are noted below and a degree of caution is advisable.

On the eastern side of Ile Grande a channel leads inshore, past the prominent rock Le Corbeau and its outlier Men Kaezh, to the seaside settlement of Landrellec. The approach is commenced from close to the Bar ar Gall buoy, using the transit shown in Figure 77. The tidal streams run across the approach and can foreshorten waves and swell to create an agitated sea. After Men Kaezh and Le Corbeau have been left about 50m to starboard, beacons mark the inner part of the channel (some of them have been omitted from the chartlet). There is a fairly deep pool off the sailing school at Porz Gélen, largely occupied by moorings but with some space to anchor on the eastern side. At neaps there will be sufficient depth to lie afloat further up the channel and nearer to Landrellec. North-east of Ile Aval, at the anchor symbol on the sketch plan, the channel dries by about 2m (MLWN is 3.5m).

For a really bombproof anchorage in rough westerly weather, the drying area between Ile Grande and Ile Aval would be hard to beat. The sand is about 4m above chart datum but there is an isolated rock that is not shown on current charts. Its tip is about 6.5m above datum (my estimate) and its approximate position is indicated on the sketch plan, just to the north-west of the anchor symbol. This rock did actually appear on the old edition of

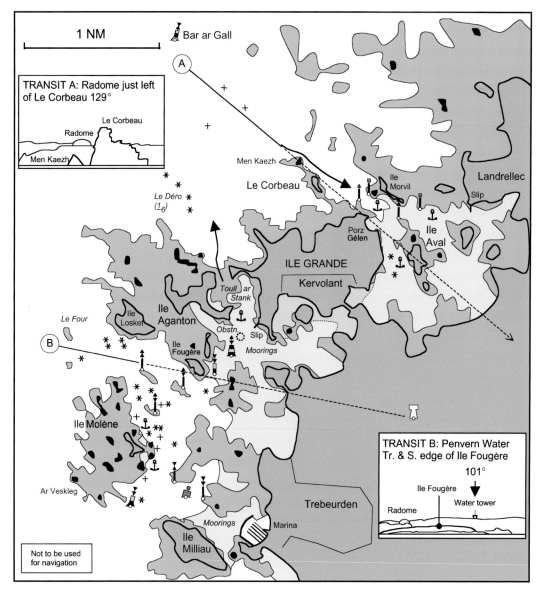

Fig 77 Around Ile Grande.

UKHO Chart 3669 but in 2003, most unusually, it was not shown on SHOM Chart 7125. It had also disappeared from the current UKHO chart because the new edition had been based on the SHOM data. Abolishing rocks by re-drawing the charts may be easier than dynamite but is less effective, as the rock is still there! Following our report, the SHOM have issued a chart correction but the UKHO chart, on a smaller scale, still shows sand.

On the western side of Ile Grande, most visiting yachts head for the marina at Trebeurden but its sill is closed at low tide. The waiting moorings, inshore of Ile Milliau, dry at low springs and are exposed to the north-west. However, around the dune-covered Ile Molène, a group of rocks and small islands uncovers at low tide, to become a solid mass

Looking south-west from Ile Grande. The yacht on the right is in the drying anchorage between Ile Grande and Ile Aganton. Note the parallel rows of oyster bed trestles (just to right of centre, in shallow water) and the old *vivier* with its twin posts, to the right of the nearer beacon.

that blocks westerly swell. Just south of its eastern corner there is a popular low water anchorage off a delicious beach, with depths shelving away to about 5m – a good spot for lingering while waiting for the marina sill to open.

Many local boats favour the eastern side of Ile Molène (see photo on back cover), although there are several rocks in this zone, most of them unmarked. At least one of them was shown on SHOM Chart 7124 as being below chart datum, but it actually dries by about 1.9m. The discrepancy may have arisen from a draughting error but it is just possible that very heavy swell could have moved large boulders on this area of sand. SHOM have now issued a chart correction. Near to low tide, in sunny conditions, the rocks should be visible underwater as black lumps against lighter sand, and the only way to be absolutely certain of avoiding any shocks is to copy the locals by steering around the lumps and anchoring between them. There is a relatively rock-free area west of Ile Fougère but this position is only sheltered in easterly winds and is open to any swell from the west.

From Ile Molène, a channel leads north-eastward to a mooring area off the south-west corner of Ile Grande. Shallow and drying rocks lie within the area of the marked channel and some oyster beds are close to its north-western side. However, the Ile Grande moorings dry by about 3m, so there is no need to head towards them until the tide has risen sufficiently. Even at this distance an inspection by binoculars ought to reveal the obstacles and a move up the channel should be delayed until they are covered by an appropriate depth. One particular obstruction is indicated on Figure 77, to the south-west of the Ile Grande slip. It is an old concrete *vivier* that was once marked by two posts. Unfortunately, the posts have crumbled and now extend to only about 6.2m above datum: just right for snaring a boat at high tide. They may be marked by a couple of plastic containers on a piece of string.

In the Toull ar Stank, between Ile Grande and Ile Aganton, there is an anchorage that dries by 4m and enjoys close shelter from all directions except south. The bottom should be checked visually, through the clear water, because there are some patches of stones and also lines of stones that are probably old fish traps. Look for the areas of clean, rippled sand.

The conventional approach to Ile Grande is from the south-west, either around the south of Ile Molène or through the shoals to its north, for which I have shown what I believe to be the best transit. When the wind is fresh and from the west, however, departing by either of these routes would be hard work. For a short cut, we have used the back door at the northern end of the Toull ar Stank, which entails steering around an S-bend and then through the narrow exit, where the best line is slightly towards the western side. The bed of the channel is generally about 4.5m above datum but is partly covered by loose rubble. MHWS is 9.2m and MHWN is 7.3m, so on most days there should be enough depth at high water but the only way to judge the line of the channel is to inspect it beforehand, at low tide.

Large waves and very heavy swell can break right across the exit but local boats use the passage under suitable conditions and we experienced no problems at heights of tide around 8m, with moderate westerly swell. A precautionary inspection can be undertaken from within the Toull ar Stank, before a decision is made to continue through the exit. The flood tide runs northward through the gap and creates abrupt overfalls where it meets waves or swell, although these decrease when the current slackens, about an hour after local high water. Once clear of the gap, the best track is towards the Bar ar Gall buoy. At around high water the main tide flows westward along the coast. If there is a westerly wind or swell, overfalls are created on the downstream sides of the rocks to the north of Ile Grande and those that extend north of Ile Aganton, including Le Déro. Under such conditions, the sea directly north of the gap and between these shoals appears to be less agitated.

On shore, Ile Grande's hamlet of Kervolant is a prosperous-looking place, with a small supermarket and a baker to serve the holidaymakers who occupy many of the houses during the summer. Fresh water can be obtained from near to the slip at the south-west corner of the island.

ILE DE BATZ TO L'ABER WRAC'H

The raw strip of coastal granite between Ile de Batz and the Abers is famous for heavy and relentless swell. Given fine weather and a flat sea, there are numerous minor coves that may be visited. More usually, there is a choice of making for L'Aberwrac'h or finding an intermediate secure anchorage with protection from wind, or swell, or both. The three best places are below.

Moguériec

THE BAY BETWEEN THE MOGUÉRIEC HARBOUR AND ILE DE SIEC is the only one on this coast with both deep water and shelter from the east. Moguériec's green and white leading marks are very distinctive and give a clear lead past the off-lying hazards, including the dangerous detached rock of Méan Nevez. During fine weather, in offshore winds and when there have been no recent depressions to stir up the Atlantic, the anchorage would be idyllic. However, it is almost completely open to westerly swell. We visited here with the wind in the south and the roadstead off the harbour apparently sheltered, only to find big rollers thumping all along the beach and smaller, distorted swells crisscrossing the roadstead. Going ashore by dinghy at low tide was impossible.

The outer part of the harbour is occupied by small boats, moored fore-and-aft. The inner part is better protected but may be occupied by larger fishing craft. I would not attempt to moor in the harbour in order to escape from swell but the jetty should be a suitable place for landing by dinghy at high tide. Provisions are available from the village.

Pontusval

THE PORT OF PONTUSVAL HAS NO DEEP WATER but has good natural breakwaters – reefs with numerous rock heads on either side of the approach. The entrance is between, on the west side, a line of three above-water rocks and on the east side, a masonry beacon followed by a rock head and a pole beacon. The three western rocks are supposedly white although, at the time of our last visit, a lack of white paint or depleted guano production had allowed them to fade.

Within the entrance and to seaward of the rock ledge Kinloc'h du Dedans, which is

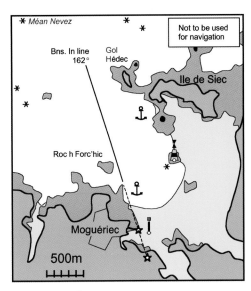

Fig 78 Moguériec.

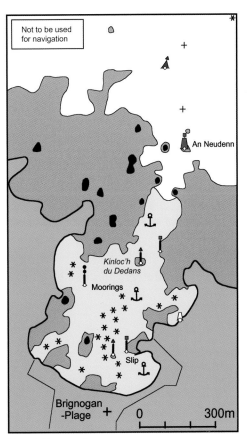

Fig 79 Pontusval.

Pontusval – the slipway in the south-east corner of the harbour, looking north towards the exposed heads of the protecting reef.

marked by a starboard-hand beacon, there is sufficient depth at neap tides for cruisers to lie afloat. Further inshore, it is invariably necessary to take the ground. In the middle of the harbour there are several large ledges of rock, with other smaller outcrops, scattered stones and small boulders. However, a wide strip of sand to the south of Kinloc'h du Dedans is fairly free of stones and moorings. On a first visit it would be sensible to anchor in this zone and then inspect the harbour bed at low water. The sand is hard and anchors should be properly dug in.

At high tide the outer reefs are effective in shredding westerly swell and the harbour is protected from all directions except north and north-east. In those conditions, it is possible to retreat into the south-east corner of the harbour, behind a small promontory with a slipway.

The harbour is overlooked by the town of Brignogan-Plage and is entirely devoted to holidaymaking. Water is available from a tap by the slip and there are several shops, including a small yacht chandler.

Corréjou

THIS LITTLE PORT HAS BOTH DEEP WATER AND DRYING ANCHORAGES, with the best shelter from the west and unusually good protection against swell. The bay once served as a refuge for sailing coasters and was protected by batteries of guns but now the main activities are sailing tuition and seaweed dredging. It seems to be rarely visited by yachts, possibly because it is surrounded by reefs, but the pilotage is straightforward and those reefs act as outer breakwaters.

There are two approach channels. The Chenal Oriental leads in from the north, marked by a port-hand buoy and a starboard-hand beacon. From the west, the Chenal Occidental runs between reefs and shore. On both the detached reefs and the foreshore rocks, certain rock heads are fairly close to the edges and help to mark the channel. These approaches converge at the Barr ar Skoaz buoy, after which inbound vessels pass through a narrow gap between a port-hand beacon and the eastern extremity of Penhers, a grass-topped island that forms the bay's inner breakwater.

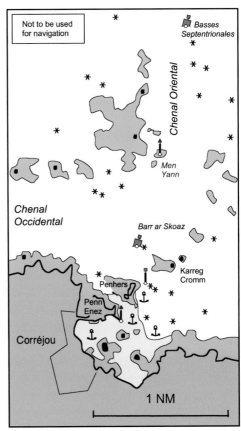

The peninsula of Penn Enez extends from the eastern shore towards Penhers, ending in a slip marked by a starboard-hand beacon. South of Penn Enez is a group of moorings and a good drying anchorage, sheltered from north, west and south. Close to the end of the slip there is sufficient depth to lie afloat at neaps. This position is partly exposed to the north, but westerly swell is considerably reduced by the time it has passed between Penn Enez and Penhers. For spring tides, there are possible deep-water anchorages close to the south-east of Penhers and near to the southern shore. Unmarked rocks extend south from Penhers, with another lump in the middle of the bay, but these are well covered at high tide and can be avoided at other times by using bearings on the two beacons.

There is a freshwater tap on Penn Enez at the sailing school building, but no local shop. However, the town of Plouguerneau is about a

Fig 80 Corréjou.

mile inland. For yachts moored at L'Aber Wrac'h, shopping for provisions also entails an uphill walk, so Corréjou makes a convenient alternative. It does have one drawback: it is within an area of sea that was once a minefield and charts still suggest that anchoring or fishing is potentially hazardous. I have taken the view that any undiscovered mines are likely to be further offshore and Corréjou is too good to miss, but each skipper must make his or her own decision.

L'ABER WRAC'H TO THE CHENAL DU FOUR

Yachts are discouraged from anchoring in L'Aber Wrac'h but at L'Aber Benoit it is still possible to find a sheltered spot clear of moorings, either close inside the river entrance or upstream and around the bend, off the quay at Stellac'h, taking care to avoid shellfish beds on the foreshores. Beyond L'Aber Benoit there are no deep estuary anchorages before the Rade de Brest, although L'Aberildut has hospitable moorings. If we want to lie to our own hook, we must either find shelter within the mainland reefs or head out to the islands.

The conventional mainland options are the drying inlets such as Portsall, Argenton, Melon and Porz Paul. At the first two, there is space to anchor and take the ground in

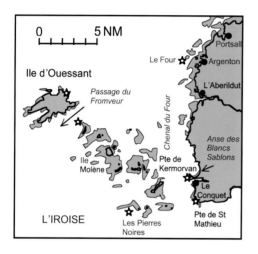

Fig 81 The approaches to the Chenal du Four.

their inner harbours, but the areas of deeper water, to seaward of the moorings, are open to the west. Fortunately, the off-lying reefs provide some protection against swell. In the other minor harbours, the best drying areas are largely filled with moored boats and the outer anchorages are only really suitable for settled conditions and offshore winds.

That leaves the Islands of the Iroise. Ile d'Ouessant has anchorages for most wind directions but it is necessary to dodge around its landmass if the wind shifts. The Baie de Lampaul is open to the Atlantic but makes a pleasant anchorage in fine weather and winds from north or east. On the other side, the gaunt Baie du Stiff is sheltered from the ocean, although big swell bounces around between its cliffs, particularly when the main tide is flowing to the east. Any passage through the Passage du Fromveur must be timed carefully because the tidal streams are very swift and can generate rough water, particularly when they flow against wind or swell. The principal shops are at Lampaul but there is a small out-of-town supermarket on the main road between Lampaul and Le Stiff, where most of the traffic consists of cyclists.

Ile Molène is the second populated island, with a clearly marked approach, a small but well organised harbour, a freshwater tap and a shop selling provisions. Few yachts visit the other islands, although both Ile de Quéménès and Ile de Béniguet have attractive anchorages. Yachts that are heading north or south generally pass through the Chenal du Four but it may be convenient to take a break among these islands, particularly if the tide is about to turn foul. In general terms, the streams run north with the flood and south with the ebb, but the island chain baulks the tidal surges and acts as a weir. The channels between the islands are the sluices, with correspondingly powerful currents pouring through them.

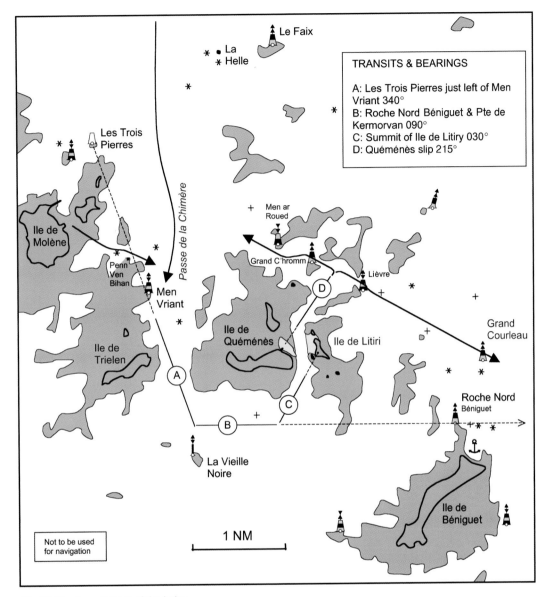

TRANSITS & BEARINGS

A: Les Trois Pierres just left of Men Vriant 340°
B: Roche Nord Béniguet & Pte de Kermorvan 090°
C: Summit of Ile de Litiry 030°
D: Quéménès slip 215°

Fig 82 The inner islands of the Iroise.

Passe de la Chimère

FOR DIVERSIONS THROUGH THE ISLANDS, the Passe de la Chimère, between Molène and Quéménès, is a useful short cut but demands a detailed chart, preferably on a scale of 1:25,000 (SHOM 7122 or UKHO 3345). To enter this channel from the north, first navigate to a position fairly close (say 200m) to the east of the Men Vriant beacon. The approach track should avoid shoals to the west of La Helle, a prominent rock stack, and also a drying rock that is about half a mile north and slightly east of the beacon. However, if the passage is made at about high water slack, in order to catch the first of the ebb, these hazards will be well submerged.

At high water, the Passe de la Chimère can also be entered directly from the harbour at Ile de Molène, by crossing the shingle bar at the eastern side of the harbour. This bar dries by nearly 4m but MHWN is 5.7m and MHWS is 7.3m. The pointed rock of Penn Ven Bihan, north-west of Men Vriant, is exposed at MHWS and makes a convenient mark. From about the middle of the bar, track directly towards Penn Ven Bihan, which should be roughly on line with the distant Pointe de St Mathieu, and then leave it about 100m to starboard, continuing to track eastward until beyond Men Vriant before turning down the Passe. Rocks on either side of this track dry by more than 4m but rocks directly below it are well covered at high tide.

From close to the Men Vriant beacon, follow Transit A as shown on the sketch plan. The Vielle Noire east cardinal beacon actually stands on the western edge of a drying ledge. When continuing further south, at high tide, there is enough depth to pass (say) 100m to the west of the beacon; at other times, pass at least 400m to its east.

The above procedures can be reversed when approaching from the south with the last of the flood, to arrive at about high water. At low tide, however, the back door to Ile

Molène is closed and the harbour must be entered from the north. The line of Transit A crosses charted depths of less than 1m, so caution is necessary when using the Passe de la Chimère at very low tides.

Ile de Quéménès

THE PASSE DU C'HROMMIG, between Quéménès and Ile de Litiri, can be entered from either end but the southern approach is probably easier for a stranger. We have used Lines B and C, as on Figure 82, entering at low water and against the last of the ebb. For the northern exit, Line D is the approximate alignment of the concrete slip on Ile Quéménès. I have drawn this exit as deeper than chart datum (which it was in 2003) but terrestrial maps show a drying sandbank across the channel, to the north of Ile Litiri. This suggests that the channel has been shallower in some years and that the sandbank may reappear in the future.

The anchorage off Ile de Litiri, with Ile de Quéménès on the right.

The routes leading out of the reef, to east and west, are via the Passe du Grand C'hromm, a narrow channel that zigzags along a row of four cardinal beacons. The finer details of the zigzag are evident from the large-scale charts, but should be studied carefully beforehand so that there is no confusion between the beacons.

Within the Passe du C'hrommig there is a beautiful anchorage close to Ile de Litiri, on a ledge of coarse granite sand that dries by about 1.1m (average). MLWS is 1.1m and MLWN is 2.8m, so this is ideal for neap tides, when most yachts will just lie afloat at low water. At springs, it could be a good drying anchorage but only in the absence of swell. The flood stream runs just clear of the ledge but the ebb runs across it until the rocks to the north become uncovered. On the other side of the Passe, Ile de Quéménès is private but an area of sand, close to its slip, dries by about

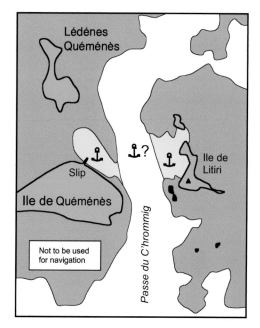

Fig 83 Anchorages between Ile de Quéménès and the Ile de Litiri. (Note: the anchorage in the channel is stubject to strong currents.)

2m. The island's resident told us that in south-west winds this position is one of the most sheltered anchorages within the islands. In the middle of the Passe the bottom is less satisfactory – weed on rock with patches of sand, and the streams run very fast, although the turbulence tends to flatten the water. This anchorage position may be tenable at spring tides, provided that the anchor is embedded in the sand and checked at each reversal of the current.

Ile de Béniguet

ON A CHART, THE SMALL BIGHT at the northern end of Ile de Béniguet looks unimpressive but it is a very elegant anchorage, enclosed within a splendid arc of white pebbles and just out of the main tidal streams. On each side, ledges extend northward from the island and there are some isolated rocks (one drying by 3.7m) about 500m to the north. However, it is not difficult to enter and leave on the eastern side, possibly using a check transit of Roche Nord Béniguet beacon in line with the houses on Ile Molène. Within the anchorage parts of the bottom are covered by less than 2m at LAT, so caution is advisable at low spring tides.

Three miles to the east, on the mainland, the extravagantly curved Anse des Blancs Sablons appears to offer perfect shelter from the south; nevertheless, we have anchored there in a southerly wind while heavy swell rolled into the bay from the north-west and thundered on the beach, having apparently refracted around Ushant. It is noticeable that there are no moorings in the southern part of the bay and all the local boats hide in smaller bays that are protected from the north-west. A little earlier, the bight on Ile de

The anchorage in the bight at the northern end of Ile de Béniguet.

Béniguet had been slightly agitated by small waves interacting with the strong currents on either side, but as an anchorage it had been far more comfortable.

The middle of Béniguet, which used to be farmed, is now a nature reserve but there are no restrictions on walking along the beaches. The powerful tides of the Chenal du Four sluice past the island and boil over the shoals, and yet they have always been a predictable part of the local transport system. This was once the working environment of the *Chasse Marée* sailing coasters, when lug-rigged vessels would have called at the farm's landing place on the eastern shore, or might have anchored in the northern bight to await a south-going stream. Yachts now ride by on the currents, heading north or south between the English Channel and the Bay of Biscay, but few of their crews pause to explore these minor islands or the coastal inlets that they glimpse while on passage. They are missing some treats.

17 Where Next?

When we have explored the anchorages and navigable inlets of the western English Channel, it will be tempting to continue southward, through the Chenal du Four. The weather of southern Brittany is usually warmer and there is another good selection of islands, bays and estuaries. In July and August the islands and their harbours become extremely crowded, and so most cruising yachts use the open anchorages as a matter of course. The sea breeze cycle can create problems because hot weather usually generates an afternoon breeze from the west or WNW. Yachts cluster in east-facing bays but then suffer an uncomfortable night if, as often happens, a nocturnal wind comes from the north-east. This is popularly known as the *Vent Solaire*, although it appears to be a recurrence of the gradient wind rather than a true thermal land breeze. Numerous alternative anchorages are available in the estuaries, including the large inland seas of the Rade de Brest and Golfe du Morbihan, and these are relatively deserted when all the local yachts have gone out to the islands.

If we choose to turn north rather than south, the east coast of England is one option but most of its well-sheltered anchorages are inside the river estuaries that lie close to the Thames. The Irish Sea has more indented shorelines, with some particularly notable coastal bays and estuaries in both south and north Wales. The Pembrokeshire coastal park boasts the best scenery but is subject to the same Atlantic swell as the western extremities of Cornwall and Brittany, so that flopper stopper will come in useful.

And then there is the west coast of Scotland, where superlative scenery is guaranteed, although the weather is less reliable. On our last visit to the Hebrides, blue water cruising in the morning was often followed by grey water cruising after lunch, as the mountains stirred the winds to create clouds and showers. Nevertheless, occasional dampness is an acceptable price to pay for unforgettable moments, such as sailing close alongside huge cliffs of basalt, escorted by squadrons of puffins, or lying at anchor in a tranquil pool surrounded by pines, as an inquisitive seal noses around the boat. In Scotland, anchoring overnight is the rule rather than the exception, and a book such as this would be redundant because the established cruising guides were first written when there were very few marinas or moorings. Pilotage makes extensive use of friendly rocks, because in many places there are few other aids of any kind. A crew that is familiar with the wilder havens of the English Channel, on a yacht that is well equipped for life at anchor, should feel quite at home in these waters – or anywhere else, for that matter.

Good cruising!

Index